The Land Law of German New Guinea

A Collection of Documents

Peter and Bridget Sack

First published by Australian National University in 1975

Reprinted with permission by the University of Papua New Guinea Press in 2013

ISBN 978-9980-87-911-0

University of Papua New Guinea Press and Bookshop
PO Box 413
University PO, NCD
Papua New Guinea

PREFACE

Disputes regarding ownership of land have occupied much time in the courts of what is now Papua New Guinea.

Apart from disputes between persons claiming customary ownership, there have been many notable challenges to titles based on transactions which occurred at about the turn of the century when land was ostensibly acquired by government authority either as ownerless land or from the apparent indigenous owners.

When such a transaction has been challenged, the courts have faced a formidable task, especially in the area formerly known as New Guinea.

From 1886 until 1921 the law of that country, under which many of the disputed acquisitions occurred, was the German law applicable to what was first a Protectorate and later a colony of the Reich.

It is easy enough to accept that the efficacy of those transactions must be tested by reference to the law in force at the transaction but it is seldom appreciated that the courts when so acting are not applying a foreign law but what was the law of the land. Naturally enough, this creates considerable difficulties for lawyers and judges with no knowledge of the German language or of German law and necessarily they have had to rely on English translations, varying in quality, of German texts.

The difficulties have been compounded by the loss during the 1939-45 war of the court and land registration records for New Guinea.

It was thought highly desirable that the principal law library of Papua New Guinea should contain a record in English of at least a collection of the land laws which applied in New Guinea for some 35 years.

It was for this reason that Dr Peter G. Sack was commissioned by the Supreme Court Library to prepare and translate this collection. This he has done with assistance from Mrs Sack. Anyone who has studied Dr Sack's work *Land Between Two Laws* (A.N.U. Press, 1973), a careful analysis of early non-customary land acquisition in New Guinea, will appreciate that no better informed nor qualified scholar in this field could have been commissioned.

This work provides a reliable English text for those concerned with early land acquisitions in New Guinea and a record of an important part of the former law of that country.

Gresley Clarkson
Judges' Chambers
Supreme Court
Port Moresby

12th August 1974

CONTENTS

Page

ABBREVIATIONS [1]

A.L.J.	*Australian Law Journal*
A.N.U.	Australian National University
B.G.B.	Bürgerliches Gesetzbuch (*Civil Code*)
C.L.R.	*Commonwealth Law Reports* (Australia)
D.K.Bl.	*Deutsches Kolonialblatt* (Published by the German Colonial Office)
D.K.G.	*Die deutsche Kolonialgesetzgebung* (Collection of German Colonial Legislation)
ed. (eds.)	Editor(s); Edition
et al.	*et alii* (and others)
f. (ff.)	Following
Fn.	Footnote
H.W.W.A.	Hamburgisches Welt-Wirtschafts Archiv
ibid.	*ibidem* (in the same publication)
i.e.	*id est* (that is)
M.L.	Mitchell Library, Sydney
N.K.W.L.	*Nachrichten für und über Kaiser Wilhelmsland und den Bismarckarchipel* (Published by the Neu Guinea Kompagnie)
N.L.	National Library of Australia, Canberra.
No.	Number
p. (pp.)	Page(s)

[1] For details regarding the German publications see, *Bibliographical Notes* (p. 99 ff.), Nos. 1, 3, 6, 7, 8.

P.G.	*Gesetzes-Sammlung für die Königlichen Preussischen Staaten* (Gazette of the Prussian States)
P. & N.G.L.R	*Papua (and) New Guinea Law Reports*
Pr.A.G.B.G.B.	Preussisches Ausführungsgesetz zum Bürgerlichen Gesetzbuch (Prussian Statute implementing the *Civil Code*)
R.G.Bl.	*Reichsgesetzblatt* (Gazette of the German Reich)
S.	Section
Ss.	Subsection
U.P.N.G.	University of Papua New Guinea
v.	Versus
Vol. (Vols.)	Volume(s)

INTRODUCTION

German colonial law applied in New Guinea between 1886 and 1921. Today it has little practical importance. Yet it should not be disregarded. First of all it forms part of the history of Papua New Guinea, and keen historical awareness is of prime importance to a people on their way to independence and nationhood. More importantly, however, German colonial law and the metropolitan law from which it is derived can be of considerable help in shaping Papua New Guinea's future legal system – if only as an illustration for (sometimes more appropriate) alternatives to the solutions offered by the Australian colonial law at present in force.

It would thus seem most desirable to produce an authoritative edition of the complete laws of German New Guinea in English. This would be a task of some magnitude, for which the money or staff required is unlikely to be available in the near future. Moreover, it is by no means certain that a translation would be the most satisfactory way of presenting the law of German New Guinea in a usable form. It was fortunate therefore that the commission of the Supreme Court of Papua New Guinea to prepare a collection of the land laws of German New Guinea provided an opportunity of testing the possibilities and difficulties involved in such a translation project on a much smaller scale.

The selection of documents to be included in this collection proved to be no easy task, especially because it was felt to be essential to translate any chosen document in full, instead of interfering with them by extracting only certain passages. First, the land law of German New Guinea consists of two distinct periods, each with its own set of laws. Second, it frequently overlaps other areas of law. Third, it is sometimes included in general colonial legislation and often refers to German metropolitan law. Fourth, it merges in a twilight zone of 'general conditions' and 'directions' which are not laws in the strict sense, but form an important part of the 'system'.

This collection tries to cover both periods of German colonial land law and includes the most important 'general conditions' and 'directions'. On the other hand it excludes all metropolitan legislation referred to, as well as some technical colonial legislation dealing exclusively or predominantly with questions of registration procedures, surveys and costs.

The major difficulty, however, was – predictably – the translation of the selected documents. The translation of legal documents is always an almost impossible task because it involves not only the translation from one language into another, but also the 'translation' from one legal system into another. English law is in a way itself already a 'translation' of German law into English. An English 'lease' is in the same sense the English equivalent of a

German 'lease', as an English 'spade' is the equivalent of a German 'spade'. But whereas the differences between a German and an English 'spade' do not prevent anyone from calling a 'Spaten' a 'spade', the different technical implications of an English and a German 'lease' are good reasons for hesitating to translate 'Miete' (and/or 'Pacht'!) as 'lease'. Moreover, because the technical concepts 'lease' and 'Miete' are parts of different systems of law, any attempt to express in English what 'Miete' exactly means goes somehow against the grain – at least, it would require a comparative analysis of various criteria (against the background of the system as a whole) rather than a simple word for word translation. Since such a comparative analysis was obviously impracticable, it became necessary to avoid the impression that the simple translations provided should or could be read as if they were English legal texts. The spirit, if not always the letter of the German law had to be preserved, even if violating the spirit of the English language – and the temptation to explain rather than to translate had to be resisted at all costs. In other words, a semi-legal Anglo/German Esperanto had to be used. It certainly lacks beauty, but it may fulfil its purpose of preventing the deadliest of the infinite number of possible misunderstandings.

This was the principal difficulty, but there were also several minor and more specific obstacles. Some of the documents were badly drafted, there were printing errors, omissions and contradictory versions – and the terminology used in the German text was far from consistent. Still it is hoped that the final product is not altogether unpalatable and will prove to be of some interest and use.

The history of New Guinea as a German colony really begins on 17th May 1885 when an Imperial Charter was granted to the Neu Guinea Kompagnie (p. 1ff.). The area covered by this Charter was the north-eastern quarter of the New Guinea Mainland (Kaiser Wilhelmsland) and the Bismarck Archipelago. A second Charter of 13th December 1886[1] extended it to the northern Solomons including Choiseul and Isabel – which were later transferred to Great Britain as part of the Samoa Agreement of 14th November 1899.[2]

---

1 The second Charter is published in D.K.G., Vol. 1, 436, the Declaration relating to the demarcation of the German and British spheres of influence in the Western Pacific, to which it refers, ibid., 83-6.

2 D.K.G., Vol. 4, 129-32. The frequently expressed view that Germany acquired Buka and Bougainville under this agreement is erroneous.

The Neu Guinea Kompagnie administered German New Guinea until 1st April 1899, when it became a colony of the Reich as the result of an agreement of 7th October 1898 (p.5ff., see also p.11f. and 13f.).[1] The period of Imperial administration – which also extended to German Micronesia, known as the 'Island Territory' in contrast to the 'Old Protectorate' – only lasted slightly longer: it ended on 17th September 1914 when the Acting German Governor signed the terms of capitulation to the Australian expeditionary force.

The Imperial Charter of 17th May 1885 not only marks the official beginning of New Guinea's colonial history, it also forms the basis of its colonial land law. The Charter granted the Neu Guinea Kompagnie the exclusive right to acquire ownerless or native land and foreshadowed regulations to protect the native population as well as those Europeans who had already acquired land in the colony. The Charter was supplemented by a public notice issued by the Imperial Commissioner on 22nd May 1885,[2] when he announced the granting of the Charter in the colony. According to this notice all future land acquisitions by Europeans were invalid, unless they had been approved by the authorities. It also emphasised that land rights which Europeans had already acquired were to be protected. On 19th February 1886 the Imperial Commissioner issued another notice (p.4). Having already begun with a provisional registration of land claims by German nationals on a voluntary basis, he now announced that all Europeans had to notify him of their land claims before 1st May of that year.

At this stage German colonial law had not yet formally arrived in New Guinea or any other German colony. This changed on 16th April 1886 when

---

1 Between 1st November 1889 and 1st September 1892 German New Guinea had already been administered by Imperial officials, but they had exercised the political rights of the Company under its Charters and not those of the Reich, and the Company had borne the expense of the administration (see D.K.G., Vol. 1, 440-1 and 442).

2 We have not been able to find a copy of this notice. It was based on a telegram by the Chancellor of the Reich. In a Decree of 8th June 1885 the Chancellor of the Reich informed the Neu Guinea Kompagnie that he had later instructed the Imperial Commissioner to publish an amended version of this notice in the Australian press (N.K.W.L., Vol. 1, No. 1, 5). This happened in the *Sydney Morning Herald*, of 29th July 1885 (including an English translation). The German text of this amended version is also published in N.K.W.L., Vol. 1, No. 4, 1.

the *Statute Regarding the Legal Conditions in the German Protectorates*[1] came into force. It was followed by an *Ordinance Regarding the Legal Conditions in the Protectorate of the Neu Guinea Kompagnie*, of 5th June 1886[2] which became effective on 1st September 1886.

The Ordinance of 5th June 1886 referred largely to the *Statute Regarding Consular Jurisdiction*, of 10th July 1879[3] which in turn referred for the substantive civil law, including the land law, to the relevant laws of the Reich and Prussia. These laws, however, did not apply to the native population of German New Guinea, unless this was specifically directed (Section 2 of the Ordinance of 5th June 1886).

According to the original version of the *Statute Regarding the Legal Conditions in the German Protectorates* it had been impossible to adjust the German/Prussian land law to colonial conditions. It became possible by virtue of an amendment of 7th July 1887.[4] Less than two weeks later, on 20th July 1887, the *Ordinance Regarding the Acquisition of Ownership and the Charging of Land in the Protectorate of the Neu Guinea Kompagnie* (p.15ff.) was enacted. It came into force on 1st October 1887 and remained the backbone of German colonial land law in New Guinea until 1st April 1903.

The Ordinance of 20th July 1887 was still based on the principle that German/Prussian law (in particular the Prussian *Statute Regarding the Acquisition of Ownership and the Charging of Land etc.*, of 5th May 1872)[5] was to apply in German New Guinea, though, as a rule, again only to Europeans. But this principle was modified in various ways and a wide range of specific provisions was made or foreshadowed.

On 30th July 1887 the Chancellor of the Reich issued an Implementation Order for this Ordinance laying down the rules for a system of land registration which, modelled on the Prussian legislation, was to apply in German New Guinea.[6] But this Order as well as the subsequent supplementary legislation regarding the survey of land and the registration of land rights (including costs) is outside the scope of this collection.[7]

---

1 D.K.G., Vol. 1, 23-8.

2 D.K.G., Vol. 1, 442-4 (as amended by the Ordinance of 13th July 1888).

3 D.K.G., Vol. 1, 28-36

4 D.K.G., Vol. 1, 24 (Fn.).

5 P.G., 1872, 433ff.

6 D.K.G., Vol. 1, 475-89.

7 See: D.K.G., Vol. 1, 490-2; Vol. 2, 30, 165; Vol. 6, 251; Vol. 7, 46.

On 10th August 1887 the Neu Guinea Kompagnie issued detailed Directions regarding the procedures its agents were to follow when acquiring land in exercise of the Company's monopoly (p.19ff.). They remained in force until 1st July 1905 after having been amended on 24th January 1902 (for the north of New Ireland) and on 28th July 1903 (for the Neu Guinea mainland) (p.23f.). The Neu Guinea Kompagnie and later the Imperial Government also issued forms for the purchase of native land (p.25f. and 27f.).[1]

Finally, the Neu Guinea Kompagnie issued on 15th February 1888 *General Conditions for the Transfer of Land to Settlers in the Protectorate of the Neu Guinea Kompagnie* which complete the first set of documents (p.29ff.).

The second phase of colonial land law in German New Guinea began on 21st November 1902 when the *Imperial Ordinance Regarding the Rights to Land in the German Protectorates* (p.35ff.) was enacted. It did not introduce radical changes, but was rather part of an attempt to unify the laws of the various German colonies and to adjust them to important legislative changes in Germany, in particular the enactment of the *Civil Code,* of 18th August 1896.[2] The Imperial Ordinance of 21st November 1902, which replaced the Imperial Ordinance of 20th July 1887 in principle as from 1st April 1903, was still based on the view that land owned by Europeans should be governed by German law, that native land should – for the time being – continue to be governed by the traditional laws and that special regulations for the acquisition of native and ownerless land by Europeans should be enacted.

Like the Imperial Ordinance of 20th July 1887 it referred to the *Statute Regarding Consular Jurisdiction* which had been revised in the meantime (7th April 1900),[3] but still referred to German/Prussian law – the relevant sections of the *Civil Code* now taking the place of the Prussian Statute of 5th May 1872. Again the Chancellor of the Reich issued an Order in its implementation (30th November 1902),[4] which dealt primarily with details of registration and survey, although the 1902 Ordinance in contrast to that of 1887 already incorporated some of this subject matter. The subsequent technical regulations[5] remain again outside the scope of this collection

---

1 We have so far been unable to locate any forms for taking ownerless land into possession.

2 R.G.Bl., 1896, 195ff.

3 D.K.G., Vol. 5, 47-57.

4 D.K.G., Vol. 6, 10-19.

5 See: D.K.G., Vol. 7, 148; Vol. 11, 238-9.

Since the Imperial Ordinance of 21st November 1902 was to apply in all German colonies, it had to leave some room for local variations. In the case of German New Guinea these specific regulations were issued by the Governor on 22nd July 1904 (p.43ff.).

Section 3 of this Order is of special importance. It first of all corresponded with the Imperial Charter of 17th May 1885 because it reaffirmed the land acquisition monopoly of the Government. It also corresponded with the Directions regarding the acquisition of land issued by the Neu Guinea Kompagnie on 10th August 1887, as well as dealing with the transfer of land to settlers, and was thus a counterpart of the General Conditions issued by the Neu Guinea Kompagnie on 15th February 1888. Instead of covering the ground in detail, however, Section 3 gave the Governor wide discretion to determine the conditions under which ownerless or native land could be acquired and transferred to settlers, either for individual cases or by issuing general forms. Such forms were already in use when the Order came into force on 1st July 1905, but from then on they developed into a more and more elaborate system.

The core of the first set of forms was the *General Conditions for the Transfer of Land by the Treasury of German New Guinea,* of 1st April 1904 which were amended on 14th February 1907 and again on 3rd March 1910 (p.49ff.). But other more specialised forms were in use as well. Two of them, a form authorising private individuals to acquire ownerless or native land on behalf of the Treasury and a form for the purchase of native land, are included in this collection (p.53 and 54ff.).

From 1908 onwards a growing need for a more comprehensive statement of the official land policy was felt. Based on a detailed draft prepared in 1909, *Principles for the Transfer of Land in the Protectorate of German New Guinea including the Island Territory* were issued on 24th April 1912 (p.58ff.). They were soon revised and a new version was issued on 1st January 1914 (p.72ff.).

On 14th February 1903 an *Imperial Ordinance Regarding the Expropriation of Real Property in the African and Pacific Protectorates* was enacted (p.85ff.). This Ordinance dealt with the resumption of land or land rights in the public interest. According to Section 24 it applied -- unlike the Land Ordinance of 1902 – in principle to land or land rights held by natives.

Part IX of this Ordinance is of special interest. It deals with the expropriation of European owned land in favour of 'landless' natives. In implementation of this Part, the Chancellor of the Reich issued an Order on 12th November 1903 (p.96ff.), which completes the second set of documents.

LEGAL DOCUMENTS

IMPERIAL CHARTER FOR THE NEU GUINEA KOMPAGNIE, OF 17th MAY 1885*

We, Wilhelm, by the Grace of God German Emperor, King of Prussia, etc. make known and proclaim as follows:

Whereas, in August 1884, we promised our protection to a group of German subjects, which since then has adopted the name of Neu Guinea Kompagnie, for a colonial enterprise initiated by them in certain island districts in the Western part of the Pacific which are not under the sovereignty of any other power;

Whereas this Company, under the control of our Commissioner, by an expedition which it fitted out for itself, has acquired and taken into possession in these districts, harbours and sections of the coast for the purpose of cultivation and the establishment of trading stations which, on our instruction, were subsequently placed under our protection by our war-ships;

Whereas the two German trading firms which had previously established trading stations and acquired land in parts of these districts have joined the Company;

And whereas the Company, legally represented by our Privy Councillor for Commerce, Adolph von Hansemann, has now declared that it undertakes to create and maintain in the Protectorate at its own expense such administrative institutions as will serve the promotion of trade and the economic utilisation of the land as well as the establishment and strengthening of peaceful relations with the natives and their civilisation, at the same time requesting that in order to achieve these aims it be granted by means of an Imperial Charter the right to exercise local sovereignty under our sovereignty and, in addition, the exclusive right to occupy and to dispose of ownerless land and to conclude contracts regarding land and land rights with the natives, under the supervision of our Government;

We now grant the Neu Guinea Kompagnie this our Imperial Charter and confirm hereby that we have assumed sovereignty over the districts in question.

These districts are:

1. That part of the mainland of New Guinea which is not under British or Dutch sovereignty. This district, which, on application of the Company, we have permitted to be called 'Kaiser Wilhelms-Land', extends along

---

* D.K.G., Vol.1, 434-6.

the island's north-east coast from the 141st degree of east longitude (Greenwich) to a point near Mitre Rock where the 8th degree of south latitude intersects the coast, and is bounded to the south and west by a line which follows the 8th degree of south latitude to the point where it is intersected by the 147th degree of east longitude, runs from there straight in a north-westerly direction to the intersection of the 6th degree of south latitude and the 144th degree of east longitude, from there further in a west-north-westerly direction to the intersection of the 5th degree of south latitude and the 141st degree of east longitude and then follows this meridian north to the sea.

2. The islands lying off the coast of this part of New Guinea as well as the islands of the Archipelago, which so far has been called that of New Britain and which, on application of the Company, and with our authorisation, shall bear the name 'Bismarck-Archipelago', and all other islands situated north-east of New Guinea between the equator and the 8th degree of south latitude and between the 141st and 154th degree of east longitude.

We also herewith grant the said Company, in return for its undertaking to create and maintain the administrative institutions for which it has taken responsibility and to bear the costs of an adequate administration of justice, the corresponding rights of local sovereignty as well as the exclusive right to occupy and to dispose of ownerless land in the Protectorate and to conclude contracts regarding land and land rights with the natives, all this under the supervision of our Government which will enact those regulations necessary to protect the natives and to preserve rights of ownership, which were duly acquired at an earlier date.

We reserve to our Government the organisation of the administration of justice, as well as the regulation and the conduct of relations between the Protectorate and foreign Governments.

We hereby promise and order that all our officials and officers shall, by protecting and supporting the Company and its officials in all lawful undertakings, carry this our Charter into effect.

This our Imperial Charter we grant to the Neu Guinea Kompagnie on condition that it will complete its legal organisation according to the German laws at the latest within one year from the present day, that the members of its Board of Directors, or any other persons entrusted with directing its affairs, are subjects of the German Reich, and subject to future amendments of this our Charter and the regulations enacted by our Government in its implementation, as well as to any further instructions to be issued in exercise of our supreme sovereignty over the Protectorate, and which the Company must observe under pain of forfeiting its claim to our protection.

In witness thereof we have executed this our Charter with our own hand and caused to be attached to it our Imperial Seal.

Given at Berlin, 17th May 1885.

Wilhelm
Fürst v. Bismarck

(L.S.)

PUBLIC NOTICE, OF 19th FEBRUARY 1886*

In pursuance of the Ordinance which was proclaimed here on 22nd May of last year,[1] according to which

> "new land acquisitions in the German Protectorate are invalid without the approval of the German authorities and only rights which have been previously acquired in good faith shall be protected"

I herewith bring to public notice as instructed, that

> "all those who acquired rights of ownership to land in the Bismarck Archipelago before the said Public Notice (22nd May of last year), are to submit their titles to me for the purpose of examination and possible registration."

The titles are to be submitted before 1st May of this year. Sketch maps of the land acquired are to be attached, together with German translations, if the documents have been drawn up in another language.

In the case of competing claims the parties are to postpone either settling on or cultivating the land in question until a decision has been made about the titles.

Mioko, 19th February 1886

The Imperial Commissioner
(signed) G. v. Oertzen

---

* N.K.W.L., Vol. 2, No. 2, 58-9.

1 See: Fn. 1, p. ix.

CONTRACT BETWEEN THE REICH AND THE NEU GUINEA KOMPAGNIE, OF 7th OCTOBER 1898*

The following contract is made between the Chancellor of the Reich on behalf of the Reich and the Neu Guinea Kompagnie, represented by its Board of Directors:

Clause 1

The Reich resumes and shall itself exercise the local sovereignty granted to the Neu Guinea Kompagnie by the Imperial Charters of 17th May 1885 and 13th December 1886, as well as by subsequent Imperial Ordinances, over the Protectorate in the Pacific described therein, including all rights and duties appertaining thereto.

Clause 2

The Neu Guinea Kompagnie renounces in favour of the Reich the special property rights for the whole area of the Protectorate described in Clause 1 which were granted to it by the Charters and which it possesses by virtue of the same, to wit:

a) the exclusive right to occupy and to dispose of ownerless land, as well as to conclude contracts with the natives regarding land and land rights,

b) the right to make the following commercial undertakings dependent on its permission and subject to certain conditions, in particular the payment of fees: fishing for pearl-shell, pearls and trepang, exploiting deposits of guano or other fertilisers, mining for ores, precious stones and combustible minerals, exploiting coconut groves, not in the possession of natives or otherwise privately owned, for copra, coastal fishing and felling timber for commercial or trading purposes in all areas which are not privately owned.

Clause 3

The Neu Guinea Kompagnie cedes to the Reich free of charge the buildings, inventory items, harbour and shipping installations, vessels and movables used in administering the country, as shown in the attached list, in the condition in which they are at the time of the transfer. In addition to the

---

* D.K.G., Vol.5, 27-30, D.K.Bl., 1900, 279-281 (see: Fn.1, p.7).

buildings the blocks of land on which they are erected will be transferred, as well as those blocks which through their use as gardens or for other domestic purposes are attached to them. Likewise all blocks used by the Neu Guinea Kompagnie as public roads or for other public purposes shall be transferred to the Reich.

Clause 4

The Neu Guinea Kompagnie will oblige the officials employed by it in the Protectorate to take over any official duties connected with the local administration, such as the duties of police, postal, or harbour officials, court clerks, customs or tax collectors etc., in all places where no suitable Imperial officials are posted, without compensation for the personal effort involved, in so far as this is at all compatible with the duties they have to perform in the service of the Company.

The transfer of such official duties is to be preceded by an agreement with the Company's highest representative in the Protectorate; the recall of such an official on the part of the Company is to be preceded by an announcement at the earliest possible date.

The Neu Guinea Kompagnie will also make available for administrative purposes the use of its steamships serving the Protectorate, be it by way of charter for a certain time or be it for payment of personal fares and freight expenses on the ships' regular runs, both at appropriate rates, and will comply with the needs of the Administration as far as possible.

The mutual use of existing hospitals by officials and labourers, as well as the mutual granting of medical assistance shall be made as easy as possible by both parties, and the conditions for this shall be settled by special agreement.

Clause 5

By virtue of the Ordinance of 1st August 1894 the Neu Guinea Kompagnie has up to date minted 50,000 New Guinea marks in gold, 200,035 New Guinea marks in silver and 20,000 New Guinea marks in bronze or copper coins. The Company renounces the right to any further minting. The Reich reserves the right to withdraw the New Guinea coins after a certain redemption period. In this case the Neu Guinea Kompagnie is obliged to exchange the coins for an equal amount of Reich coins. If the exchange of New Guinea coins for Reich coins is not carried out by the Reich, it will refund to the Neu Guinea Kompagnie the expenses, which the latter incurs through the transport of withdrawn coins to Berlin and the return consignment of the same amount in Reich coins.

If the period of redemption expires before 1st April 1905, half of the amount received during this time shall be withdrawn at the expense of the Reich.

Until the expiry of the redemption period it shall continue to be the Neu Guinea Kompagnie's duty to write cheques for the delivery of New Guinea coins in accordance with Section 4 of its *Ordinance Regarding the Minting of New Guinea Coins,* of 1st August 1894.

Clause 6

The Reich grants the Neu Guinea Kompagnie a capital of 4,000,000 marks with the right to pay the same in ten yearly instalments of 400,000 marks each, which fall due on 1st April each year, beginning with 1st April 1899, without paying interest on the remaining amount.

The Neu Guinea Kompagnie is obliged to spend each instalment within four years on commercial undertakings in the interest of the Protectorate and has to account for the amount spent during each financial year by presenting an annual balance to the Chancellor of the Reich or a Commissioner appointed by him.

In order to ensure the functioning of these commercial undertakings, depending on local labour as they do, measures will be taken within the above period to make it easier for the Neu Guinea Kompagnie to recruit natives in Kaiser Wilhelmsland under the supervision of the Government.

Clause 7[1]

The Neu Guinea Kompagnie is also entitled to take into possession, without payment to the Reich, 50,000 hectares of land of its choice in Kaiser Wilhelmsland and the islands belonging thereto within three years from 1st

[1] The wording of this clause in D.K.G., Vol.5, 30 differs from that in D.K.Bl., 1900, 280, the former source claiming that the wording in the latter was erroneous. The confusion arises because the German Parliament amended the text of this clause after the contract had been signed. D.K.G., Vol.5, 30 reproduces the original text as signed on 7th October 1898. D.K.Bl., 1900, 280, incorporates the subsequent amendment, however, it does indeed contain a minor error. Originally the Neu Guinea Kompagnie had been entitled to select the 50,000 hectares of land granted to it within ten years, in New Britain (outside the Gazelle Peninsula) as well as Kaiser Wilhelmsland. Parliament reduced the time limit to three years and restricted the geographical area to Kaiser Wilhelmsland. D.K.Bl., 1900, 280, overlooked that in consequence of this amendment minor changes were required in subsequent, subordinate conditions and continues to speak of the "two main islands" – as opposed to the smaller off-shore islands – although the amendment had moved New Britain outside the scope of the contract. The text translated here is that reproduced in D.K.Bl., 1900, 280.

April 1899 — without prejudice to duly acquired rights of third parties — with the proviso, however, that the selection of land along the coast and river banks on the two main islands named above[1] is limited to a total sea- and river-frontage of 100 kilometres. The land to be selected along the sea or rivers must extend at least one kilometre inland, unless the natural topography of the area in question makes an adjustment necessary. Land thus acquired is subject to the provisions of an expropriation ordinance to be enacted regarding the transfer of land for public purposes. The Neu Guinea Kompagnie is obliged to inform the representative of the Reich in the Protectorate in each case of the land it has selected and to prove within one year that the selected land was, in accordance with existing laws, either occupied as ownerless or acquired from natives.

Further, the Neu Guinea Kompagnie has equipped at its own expense an expedition with the object of exploring the Ramu River and opening up the Bismarck Range as well as establishing stations for these purposes. In recognition thereof provision will be made to guarantee to the Company the exclusive right to exploit the area of the Ramu River, lying between the 5th degree of south latitude and its watershed, for precious metals and combustible minerals. The Company is to pay the Reich a fee of ten percent of the income derived from this exploitation after all expenses have been paid. Instead of receiving this fee the Reich is also free at the beginning of each new financial year to participate in the mining operations of the Company in the said area in such a way that profits and expenses are equally shared.

Clause 8

Subject to the approval of the Federal Council and Parliament this agreement becomes effective on 1st April 1899.

If, by mutual agreement, the Reich takes over officials from the service of the Company, the Neu Guinea Kompagnie will bear the expenses of their journey to the Protectorate and the Reich the cost of their subsequent return journey.

Taxes and other duties which are payable for certain periods in advance are to be shared proportionately for the period involved.

Any credited customs and other duties which were due before the 1st April 1899, as well as heirless estates for which proceedings have already been commenced, remain the property of the Neu Guinea Kompagnie.

---

1 See Fn. 1, p. 7.

For fees payable in accordance with the Order regarding the Ground Book[1] the decisive date is that on which the registration of ownership or any other judicial act took place and not the date on which the memorandum of fees was served. If the Neu Guinea Kompagnie incurred expenses in Ground Book matters instituted before 1st April 1899, which are to be refunded by the applicant, the amounts paid are due to the Neu Guinea Kompagnie. The same applies to survey fees which were due before 1st April 1899 in respect of surveys carried out at the request of private persons by the surveyor in the service of the Neu Guinea Kompagnie.

In addition the Neu Guinea Kompagnie retains all it has acquired or levied in the actual exercise of its rights and privileges before the 1st April 1899, including claims to land for which it possesses acquisition titles, although no application for registration has so far been made, but subject to an examination of the title by the Ground Book Office.

The option for 400 hectares of land on Weber Harbour in the Gazelle Peninsula which the Neu Guinea Kompagnie has contractually granted to the Catholic Mission of the Sacred Heart of Jesus is also to remain for the latter in force in relation to the Reich.

Executed in duplicate, Berlin, 7th October 1898.

The Chancellor of the Reich
(signed) Fürst zu Hohenlohe

Neu Guinea Kompagnie
(signed) A. v. Hansemann
Chairman of the Board of Directors

(signed) E. Russell
Member of the Board of Directors

---

1 The German original uses the term 'Grundbuchordnung' in an almost colloquial sense. The official title was *Implementation Order of the Chancellor of the Reich for the Imperial Ordinance of 20th July 1887 Regarding the Acquisition of Ownership and the Charging of Land in the Protectorate of the Neu Guinea Kompagnie,* of 30th July 1887.

Enclosure (List for Clause 3 of the Contract)

Friedrich Wilhelmshafen

Buildings:

1. Administrator's residence
2. Secretary's residence
3. One office building

– All buildings including the water tanks belonging thereto –

Harbour Installations and Boats:

Wharf with two pontoons and harbour equipment (beacons, lanterns etc.), two gigs, flags.

Inventory:

Arms and equipment of the police force, Ground Books, legal library.

Herbertshöhe

Buildings:

1. Judge's house
2. Imperial court buildings, including contents
3. Court clerk's house
4. Police sergeant's house
5. Police compound
6. One prison building, including contents.

– All buildings including the water tanks belonging thereto –

Harbour Installations and Boats:

1 whaleboat, 1 gig, 2 floating beacons, divers boat parts, sails,
1 flagpole, flag-ropes, harbour lanterns, 3 flags.

Inventory:

Ground Books, legal library, equipment of the police force.

IMPERIAL ORDINANCE REGARDING THE ASSUMPTION OF LOCAL SOVEREIGNTY OVER THE PROTECTORATE OF GERMAN NEW GUINEA BY THE REICH, OF 27th MARCH 1899*

We, Wilhelm, by the Grace of God German Emperor, King of Prussia etc. order by virtue of the *Statute Regarding the Legal Conditions in the German Protectorates* (R.G.Bl., 1888, 75) in the name of the Reich as follows:

Section 1

The Reich shall assume local sovereignty over the Protectorate of German New Guinea as from 1st April 1899.

Our Charters granted by us to the Neu Guinea Kompagnie on 17th May 1885 and 13th December 1886, as well as our *Ordinance Regarding the Jurisdiction of the Neu Guinea Kompagnie over the Natives in its Protectorate,* of 15th October 1897 shall become ineffective.

Section 2

Those special property rights and other privileges which the Neu Guinea Kompagnie held by virtue of the Charters and other statutory provisions shall as from 1st April 1899 pass to the Treasury of the Protectorate of German New Guinea (*Statute Regarding the Revenue and Expenditure of the Protectorates,* of 30th March 1892, R.G.Bl., 1892, 369), except where specifically reserved to the Company by way of agreement.

Section 3

The statutory provisions which, according to Section 2 of the *Statute Regarding the Legal Conditions in the German Protectorates,* would apply to mining rights shall not be applicable. The Chancellor of the Reich and, with his approval, the Governor shall be, for the time being, authorised to regulate this matter.

Section 4

The Chancellor of the Reich is to issue the orders necessary to implement this Ordinance.

---

* D.K.G., Vol. 4, 50-1.

Section 5

This Ordinance shall come into effect on 1st April 1899.

Executed with our own hand and under the Imperial Seal.
Given at Berlin in the Castle, 27th March 1899.

(signed) Wilhelm I.R.
(signed) Fürst zu Hohenlohe

IMPLEMENTATION ORDER FOR THE IMPERIAL ORDINANCE REGARDING THE ASSUMPTION OF LOCAL SOVEREIGNTY OVER THE PROTECTORATE OF GERMAN NEW GUINEA BY THE REICH, OF 1st APRIL 1899*

By virtue of Section 4 of the Imperial Ordinance of 27th March 1899, I order for the Protectorate of German New Guinea as follows:

Section 1

In accordance with Section 2 of the said Imperial Ordinance in particular the following property rights hitherto exercised by the Neu Guinea Kompagnie shall pass to the Treasury of the Protectorate of German New Guinea:

a) the exclusive right to occupy and to dispose of ownerless land, as well as to make contracts with the natives regarding land and land rights
b) the right to make the following commercial undertakings dependent on permission from the authorities: fishing for pearl shell, pearls and trepang, exploiting deposits of guano or other fertilisers, mining for ores, precious stones and combustible minerals, exploiting coconut groves, not in the possession of natives or otherwise privately owned, for copra, coastal fishing and felling timber for commercial or trading purposes on all lands which are not privately owned.

Section 2

The entire judicial and administrative authority of the Administrator of the Protectorate of the Neu Guinea Kompagnie passes to the Imperial Governor of German New Guinea.

The Governor is empowered to issue police and other administrative regulations and to make breaches punishable by imprisonment of up to three months, custody, fines and the confiscation of individual objects.

The Chancellor of the Reich is entitled to amend or to repeal regulations issued by the Governor.

The regulations are to be proclaimed in corresponding application of the last Subsection of Section 4 of the *Statute Regarding Consular Jurisdiction*, of 10th July 1879 (R.G.Bl., 1879, 197). Unless another date is specifically set, the regulations shall become effective on their proclamation.

---

* D.K.G., Vol.4, 91. The date given there is 27th March 1899 – that is the date of the Imperial Ordinance itself – but this is clearly a mistake.

Section 3

In those cases where, according to existing laws, the participation of officers of the Company was required, Imperial officials take the place of the Company's officers.

Section 4

This order shall become effective immediately.

Berlin, 1st April 1899

The Chancellor of the Reich
(signed) Fürst zu Hohenlohe

ORDINANCE REGARDING THE ACQUISITION OF OWNERSHIP AND THE CHARGING OF LAND IN THE PROTECTORATE OF THE NEU GUINEA KOMPAGNIE, OF 20th JULY 1887*

We, Wilhelm, by the Grace of God German Emperor, King of Prussia etc., by virtue of Section 3 of the *Statute Regarding the Legal Conditions in the German Protectorates* in the wording of the Statute of 7th July 1887 (R.G.Bl., 1887, 307), order in the name of the Reich as follows:

Section 1

The acquisition of ownership and the charging of land in the Protectorate of the Neu Guinea Kompagnie, in so far as the following does not provide otherwise, shall be governed by the rules of Prussian law, in particular by the *Statute Regarding the Acquisition of Ownership and the Charging of Land, Mines and Independent Land Rights,* of 5th May 1872 (P.G., 1872, 433-445).

Section 2

The declarations by which the registered owner and the new acquirer transfer ownership (Section 2 of the *Statute Regarding the Acquisition of Ownership,* of 5th May 1872) can also be made in writing. The declarations do not have to be made contemporaneously.

Section 3

The provisions regarding land charges and the ownership of mining rights in the *Statute Regarding the Acquisition of Ownership,* as well as the *Land Registration Act,* of 5th May 1872 are not applicable.

The requisite regulations in lieu of the latter for the implementation of this Ordinance will be issued by the Chancellor of the Reich after hearing the Neu Guinea Kompagnie's Board of Directors.

Section 4

The preceding Sections apply neither to the acquisition of ownerless land nor to the land belonging to the natives. However, land which has been entered into the Ground Book remains governed by Sections 1 to 3, even if it becomes the property of a native.

---

* D.K.G., Vol.1, 469-71.

Section 5

The principles governing the acquisition of land by means of contracts with the natives or by occupying ownerless land, which is by virtue of the Imperial Charter of 17th May 1885 the exclusive right of the Neu Guinea Kompagnie, shall be laid down by the Neu Guinea Kompagnie with the approval of the Chancellor of the Reich.

Land acquired by the Neu Guinea Kompagnie in this way shall be registered in the Ground Book by virtue of an acquisition certificate issued by the Administrator or an official authorised by him.

Section 6

Other persons can only claim rights based on the occupation of ownerless land or on contracts with natives regarding the acquisition or charging of land, if the acquisition took place prior to 21st May 1885.

Section 7

The following rules shall apply to the acquisition of ownership as defined in Section 6:

In the case of the occupation of ownerless land the claim to ownership is valid only if the ownerless land was in fact occupied before 21st May 1885 and if its possession has not since been relinquished or otherwise lost.

In the case of acquisition based on contracts with natives, it shall be required that prior to 21st May 1885 a contract was concluded in writing or orally between the owner and the acquirer with the intention of transferring and acquiring ownership and that possession has been transferred and not since relinquished or otherwise lost.

Section 8

Section 7, Subsection 3 is correspondingly applicable to a transfer of land which took place between non-natives before this Ordinance comes into force.

Section 9

For the islands of the Solomons Group which belong to the Protectorate, the 28th of October 1886 shall take the place of the date set in Sections 6 and 7.

Section 10

Persons wishing to claim ownership of land in the Protectorate of the Neu Guinea Kompagnie on the basis of acquisition titles of the kind defined in Section 6 must apply to have their ownership registered in the Ground Book no later than 1st March 1888. Any claims to ownership which have not been lodged with the application described above by this date become *ipso iure* invalid.

This does not apply to claims to ownership based on titles which were registered before this Ordinance comes into force in the 'Ground Book or Register of Land Acquisition', established by the Imperial Commissioner.

Such claimants can however, on application by the Station Manager in whose district the land is situated, be summoned by the competent Ground Book Office to apply for the registration of their ownership in the new Ground Book. In such cases each claimant must be given by special order a least three months' notice and be notified that his claims will become invalid if he fails to apply in time.

Section 11

In cases falling under Section 10 a copy of the application for registration of ownership with enclosures must be sent to the Manager of the Station in whose district the land is situated, together with the request that any objections to the acquisition which might arise out of the Neu Guinea Kompagnie's exclusive right to acquire land be lodged within a set period of not more than three months.

If such objections are lodged within the set period, the applicant has to be notified and informed that he must assert his claims against the Neu Guinea Kompagnie by taking court action within a prescribed period of six months.

If the Neu Guinea Kompagnie does not lodge any objections within the set period the land will be registered, provided the examination of the acquisition title of the applicant and any predecessors (Sections 7 and 9) shows that it is otherwise valid.

In order to supplement the evidence, the Ground Book Office can make appropriate investigations and issue a public summons that it is to be notified of all claims impairing the application. A period of at least three months is to be set for the notification. The summons is to be made public by displaying it on the Court notice-board.

The Ground Book Office can dispense with the measures described in the preceding Subsection if the applicant and any predecessors have been in undisturbed possession of the land in question for at least the three preceding years.

Section 12

The provisions contained in No. IV of the *Declaration Relating to the Reciprocal Freedom of Trade and Commerce in the German and British Possessions and Protectorates in the Western Pacific,* of 10th April 1886 are not affected by Sections 7ff. The last Subsection of Section 10 applies however, as soon as the claims of a British subject have been established by the mixed Commission envisaged in No. IV of the Declaration.

Section 13

The provisions contained in this Ordinance shall not prejudice the issue of regulations introducing restrictions of ownership, for the protection of the natives, or otherwise in the public interest.

Section 14

This Ordinance shall become effective on 1st October 1887.

Executed with our own hand and under the Imperial Seal.
Given at Bad Gastein, 20th July 1887.

(L.S.)

Wilhelm
Graf v. Bismarck

DIRECTIONS REGARDING THE PROCEDURES FOR THE ACQUISITION OF LAND BY THE NEU GUINEA KOMPAGNIE, OF 10th AUGUST 1887*

By virtue of Section 5 of the Imperial Ordinance of 20th July 1887 (R.G.Bl., 1887, 379) and with the approval of the Chancellor of the Reich, the following directions are given for the occupation of ownerless land and for the acquisition of land from the natives, which, by virtue of the Imperial Charter of 17th May 1885, is the exclusive right of the Neu Guinea Kompagnie.

I. Regarding Ownerless Land

Section 1

Occupation is to be preceded by a thorough investigation as to whether the land which is to be occupied is cultivated or otherwise used by natives, or whether it is marked in a customary way as belonging to an individual or a community and whether ownership is consequently claimed by certain persons.

Section 2

If inspection reveals such signs, the persons making claims to the land in question and the nature of these claims must be ascertained by questioning the natives living nearby, especially the heads of families, communities or other groupings, if they exist. If possible an interpreter, speaking the language of the persons involved, should be called in for the questioning and subsequent discussions, which are to be recorded in a way which shows the course of the investigations and in particular the questions and answers relating to the establishing of the claims.

Land thus claimed is, for the time being, to be excluded from occupation and directions must be obtained as to whether or not negotiations for transfer of the land should be opened with the persons allegedly entitled to the land. In the former case the rules laid down in Section 5ff. are to be applied.

Section 3

If no signs can be found that the land is in the possession of natives, or if it is impossible to determine the significance of existing signs, because no natives live in the vicinity or because no explanation can be obtained from them, the observations made as well as attempts to obtain an explanation are to be

---

* D.K.G., Vol.1, 472-5.

recorded in detail, whereupon the land should be forthwith occupied.

Section 4

The occupation shall take place by positioning boundary posts, stones, fences or other signs which show that the land has been taken into possession for the Neu Guinea Kompagnie, and to what extent. This process is to be recorded and the record must show:

a) the position of the occupied land, indicating any natural boundaries, the natural condition of the soil or the extent of any cultivation, and its approximate size;
b) the number, type and kind of markings which have been used to signify that it has been occupied.

This record must carry the signature of the authorised official. A sketch map is to be attached, showing as precisely as possible the position of the land, if possible in relation to fixed points, and the boundary marks which have been erected.

II. Indirect Acquisition of Native Land

Section 5

If land is to be acquired which is in the possession of natives or which individual natives or native communities claim as belonging to them, and if the possessor(s) is (are) prepared to transfer it, the transfer is to be certified in a written contract. This is to be preceded by investigations as to which person(s) is (are), in the opinion of the natives involved, entitled to decide on the permanent disposal of the land, which procedures for such a transfer are customary among them and must be followed to render the transfer valid, and to which persons the purchase price must be paid in order to discharge the acquirer from his stipulated obligations.

If the investigation reveals that the right of disposal or the right to receive the purchase price is held by several persons, or that the disposal on the part of an individual private possessor is valid only with the approval of other persons, who belong to the possessor's family, community or a similar grouping, then *all* persons involved are to be included in the negotiations; if possible in the form of a meeting with them; or, if this is not possible, a date is to be fixed by which the transferor is to procure the approval of all other rightholders.

Section 6

Once agreement has been reached regarding the object of the acquisition and the price payable for it, as well as regarding the persons who hold the right of disposal and the right to receive the price, two identical copies of the contract are to be drawn up with the entitled persons in the German language.

This contract must include everything which, according to German law, is essential for a contract of purchase and sale or exchange, to wit in particular:

a precise description of the block of land to be transferred, indicating position, size, condition and boundaries, in such a way that it can be easily located and distinguished from other blocks,

the intention of one party to transfer the ownership and the intention of the other to accept this transfer,

the statement of the purchase or exchange price and the determination as to when and to whom it shall be paid or has been paid,

the declaration that the land has been or shall be delivered, and at what time.

The contract must also show that the significance of the transfer has been made clear to the transferor, i.e. that by the transfer he renounces for himself and his family for all time all rights to the land, and that he accordingly cannot transfer it again to any other person, whereas the new acquirer is entitled to use it or to dispose of it as he wishes.

Section 7

The contract has to be signed by the representative of the Neu Guinea Kompagnie. The native party (parties), so long as they cannot write, must affix their marks, and it must be explained to them that by doing so they make their consent final and binding. Care must also be taken that any possible co-owners, usufructuaries as well as persons whose approval is required for the transfer, sign the contract after receiving the same explanation and in the same way.

Section 8

Wherever possible, an interpreter who knows the language of the transferor(s) is to be called in and his participation must be indicated in the document. There must also be a witness, who must be present during the negotiations and who must, in particular, certify that, in his opinion, the significance of the transfer has been brought to the knowledge of the transferor. If for any reason the transferor(s) object to the affixing of their marks, although there is no doubt that they agree in substance, the reason for their objection must be stated and shown in the document. Nevertheless the contract is valid if the witness present confirms that the objection to the execution has grounds other than the lack of agreement, and that, according to his observation, agreement had been reached.

Section 9

The delivery of the acquired land must be effected in such a way that it actually takes place as soon as agreement on the contents of the contract has been reached. This and in what way it was brought about must be shown in the contract. In the exceptional case of delivery taking place at a later date, this must be recorded in writing in a separate document for which the same form as for the contract of transfer must be observed.

Section 10

As a rule the payment of the purchase price in money or goods shall take place immediately after the delivery of the land. It is the strict duty of the Company's representatives to make sure that the price is paid without any deductions and in full accordance with the previous agreement to those persons who are entitled to it, as shown by the preceding investigations. If there are several persons so entitled, the dividing up of the purchase price is to be left to them. The contract is to indicate that payment has been made, the persons who received it, acknowledgement of receipt and the fact that all claims against the acquirer have been satisfied. If, for special reasons, the payment of the purchase price takes place at a date later than that of the execution of the contract, this is to be recorded in a separate document for which the same forms as for the contract must be observed.

Section 11

Once the contract has been executed, one of the two copies is to be handed over to and remain with the transferor(s).

Berlin, 10th August 1887.

Neu Guinea Kompagnie
The Board of Directors:

A. v. Hansemann. Herzog
Chairman

NOTICE BY THE GOVERNOR OF GERMAN NEW GUINEA REGARDING THE ACQUISITION OF OWNERLESS AND NATIVE LAND, OF 28th JULY 1903*

In further implementation of the *Directions Regarding the Procedures for the Acquisition of Land by the Neu Guinea Kompagnie*, of 10th August 1887, by virtue of Section 3 of the *Imperial Ordinance Regarding the Legal Conditions in the German Protectorates*, of 9th November 1900, I order, for the area under the jurisdiction of the court in Friedrich Wilhelmshafen as follows:

I. Regarding Ownerless Land, Section 4 of the Directions

The occupation of such land can only be effected and certified by the Imperial District Commissioner in Friedrich Wilhelmshafen or by persons authorised by him.

II. Indirect Acquisition of Native Land

Only the Imperial District Commissioner in Friedrich Wilhelmshafen or a person specifically authorised by him is entitled to conclude contracts of purchase and sale for the Imperial Government (Treasury of the Protectorate of German New Guinea). Other persons who have obtained permission from the Imperial Government for the purchase of land in the possession of natives must therefore refer to the Imperial District Commissioner for the execution of their contracts of purchase and sale.

III. Reserve of the Neu Guinea Kompagnie

The right of the Neu Guinea Kompagnie to acquire land directly in the reserve granted to it remains unaffected; viz:

---

* D.K.G., Vol.7, 171-2. A similar notice had been issued for the District of the Imperial Station in Nusa (Northern New Ireland) on 24th January 1902 (ibid., Fn. which shows the (minor) differences in the wording of these notices).

3,000 hectares on the southern point of Rook Island,

2,000 hectares on the lower reaches of the Nuru (Elisabeth River),

1,000 hectares on the Ramu River, upper reaches; Goldfield Station,

2,000 hectares on the Franziska River.

Herbertshöhe, 28th July 1903

The Imperial Governor
Hahl

FORM FOR CONTRACT OF PURCHASE AND SALE, ISSUED BY THE NEU GUINEA KOMPAGNIE, OF ABOUT 1888*

Between

1. the Neu Guinea Kompagnie of Berlin, represented by . . .

and

2. . . .
   assisted by . . . .

The following contract of purchase and sale has been made on this . . . day of the year . . . at . . . .

Clause 1

The person(s) named above under 2. sell(s) and transfer(s) to the Neu Guinea Kompagnie the block(s) of land described below

1. . . . [description of the land]

including all trees, gardens and buildings thereon for the price of . . . which is to be paid to him (them) in accordance with the agreement reached.

The vendor(s) affirm(s) that the block(s) of land sold has (have) hitherto been his (their) exclusive property, that he (they) also hold(s) the exclusive right to dispose of it (them) and that he (they) alone is (are) entitled to receive the agreed purchase price.

It has been explained to him (them) and understood by him (them) that, by transferring the block(s) of land and accepting the purchase price for it (them), he (they) renounce(s) all claims to it (them) for himself (themselves) and his (their) family (families), so that he (they) can neither take possession of it (them) again nor sell it (them) again, but that, on the contrary, only the purchaser will henceforth be entitled to use and dispose of it (them).

Clause 2

In accordance with the agreement reached the purchase price has been handed over to . . . . He (they) acknowledge(s) the receipt and declare(s) that all his (their) claims have thereby been satisfied.

---

* This form was not published in any of the collections of German colonial laws; a photocopy of the original on which this translation is based has been deposited in the library of the Supreme Court of Papua New Guinea.

Conversely the block(s) of land sold has (have) been delivered by . . . [description of the way in which the delivery was effected] and the representative of the Neu Guinea Kompagnie affirms for his part that the delivery has taken place.

In witness thereof the above contract shall be signed and sealed by the representative of Neu Guinea Kompagnie and marked by the vendor(s) as follows, after it has been made clear to him (them) that he (they) thereby make(s) his (their) consent final and binding.

In addition to the vendor(s) his (their) assistants have, after the same explanation, affixed their (signature) mark below.

. . . . [mark(s)]

. . . has been present as interpreter at the proceedings which are recorded in the contract, and . . . as witness.

The latter confirms with his signature that the proceedings have taken place as recorded and in particular that he is convinced that the transferor(s) has (have) been made aware of the significance of the transfer of ownership.

. . . . [signature]

This contract has been drawn up in two identical copies, one of which has been handed over to the vendor(s).

. . . . [signature]
Station Manager

FORM FOR CONTRACT OF PURCHASE AND SALE, ISSUED BY THE IMPERIAL GOVERNMENT, OF ABOUT 1900*

Between

1. the Imperial Government in Herbertshöhe
   represented by . . .

and

2. . . .
   assisted by . . . .

The following contract of purchase and sale has been made on this . . . day of the year . . . at . . . .

Clause 1

The person(s) named under 2. sell(s) and transfer(s) to the Imperial Government the block(s) of land described below . . . [description of the land]
including all trees, gardens and buildings thereon for the price of . . . which is to be paid to him (them) in accordance with the agreement reached.

The vendor(s) affirm(s) that the block(s) of land sold has (have) hitherto been his (their) exclusive property, that he (they) also hold(s) the exclusive right to dispose of it (them) and that he (they) alone is (are) entitled to receive the agreed purchase price.

It has been explained to him (them) and understood by him (them) that, by transferring the block(s) of land and accepting the purchase price for it (them), he (they) renounce(s) all claims to it (them) for himself (themselves) and his (their) family (families), so that he (they) can neither take possession of it (them) again nor sell it (them) again, but that, on the contrary, only the purchaser will henceforth be entitled to use and dispose of it (them).

Clause 2

In accordance with the agreement reached the purchase price has been handed over to . . . . He (they) acknowledge(s) the receipt and declare(s) that all his (their) claims have thereby been satisfied.

---

* This form was not published in any of the collections of German colonial laws; a photocopy of the original on which this translation is based has been deposited in the library of the Supreme Court of Papua New Guinea.

Conversely the block(s) of land sold has (have) been delivered and the representative of the Government affirms for his part that the delivery has taken place.

In witness thereof the above contract has been executed by both parties as follows, by the vendor(s), after it was made clear to him (them) that he (they) thereby make(s) his (their) consent final and binding.

. . . . [mark(s)]

In addition to the vendor(s), his (their) assistants have, after the same explanation, affixed their (signature) mark below.

. . . . [marks]

As witness(es) was (were) present . . . .

He (they) confirm(s) with his (their) signature that the proceedings have taken place as recorded and in particular that he (they) is (are) convinced that the transferor(s) has (have) been made aware of the significance of the transfer of ownership.

. . . . [place, date, signatures of purchaser and witness(es).

GENERAL CONDITIONS FOR THE TRANSFER OF LAND TO SETTLERS IN THE PROTECTORATE OF THE NEU GUINEA KOMPAGNIE, OF 15th FEBRUARY 1888*

Section 1

Land available for transfer is divided into:

a) urban land, that is land in areas intended for the development of townships and demarcated for this purpose, and

b) rural land outside such areas.

Section 2

For all blocks there shall either be maps available which have been drawn up in accordance with the Order regarding the Ground Book[1] of 30th July 1887, or their location and size shall be clearly defined by a description and by boundary marks on the site itself.

Section 3

In each Station in the Protectorate in whose district land is available for transfer, a list of the blocks with all necessary details shall be open for inspection.

Section 4

Land offered for selection shall either be

a) transferred into ownership by outright purchase or

b) leased for five years, the lessee having an option to purchase the selected block at any time during the period of the lease for a predetermined price, or

c) leased without an option to purchase.

The public list (Section 3) shall show for each block which of the above forms of transfer is available.

Urban land shall, as a rule, be transferred only under the conditions set out under a).

The term 'year' is used above in the sense of a calendar year. The current year in which the transfer takes place does not count towards the period of the lease.

---

* N.K.W.L., Vol.4, 2-8.

1 See: Fn., 1, p. 9.

Section 5

Application for the transfer of land is to be made to the Administrator or to the Station Manager in whose district it is situated. Forms A, B, or C[1] must be used, depending on whether the land is transferable under the conditions set out in Section 4, Letters a), b) or c).

Section 6

On submitting his application (Section 5) the applicant shall be obliged to make the following payments:

a) in the case of a purchase (Section 4, a) one-tenth of the purchase price as a deposit,

b) in the case of a lease with an option to purchase (Section 4, b) the rent for the following calendar year which will be one-tenth of the pre-determined purchase price, and a proportionate amount for the current year, as well as the survey fee,

c) in the case of a lease without the option to purchase (Section 4, c) the rent for the following calendar year and a proportionate amount for the current year.

The payments are to be made to the pay-office of the Central Station in Finschhafen or to the pay-office of the respective local Station.

Section 7

The Administrator or the authorised Station Manager shall decide whether the application is to be accepted or rejected. In the case of a rejection, for which no reasons need be given, the advance payments (Section 5) shall be returned with the rejection notice. An acceptance shall be confirmed in accordance with Forms D, E or F[1] which correspond to the different applications.

This confirmation, together with the application, forms the contract between the settler and the Company regarding the land transferred. The confirmation at the same time authorises the applicant to take into possession the land indicated therein.

Section 8

In all cases the Administrator is entitled to auction land publicly before confirming an application for its purchase or lease. The highest bidder then takes the place of the applicant.

---

1 The Forms A-F (N.K.W.L., Vol.4, 9-14) have not been translated as they do not contain additional information.

Section 9

If an application for purchase (Section 4, a) has been accepted, the full purchase price, after the deposit has been credited, as well as the survey fee is to be paid on delivery of the confirmation within eight days of the latter being announced, failing which the deposit shall be forfeited and the application shall be deemed to have been rejected.

If the purchase price (Section 4, a and b) amounts to more than 600 marks the purchaser is entitled, instead of paying the full amount, to pay half of it as a deposit and to pay the rest in yearly instalments of at least one-tenth of the purchase price. The instalments are due on the 31st December of each year. In conjunction with them, interest of 5 per cent per annum on the outstanding part of the purchase price is to be paid. Interest on the outstanding part of the purchase price, which is to be entered in the Ground Book, is payable as from the calendar month in which the application for purchase is confirmed. In the case of a purchase with preceding lease (Section 4, b) interest is payable as from the calendar year in which the payment of rent is terminated.

Section 10

As soon as the full purchase price has been paid or half of it, if this is permissible under Section 9, the real conveyance of the land to the purchaser will take place.

Section 11

The stamp-duty on the contracts, the cost of maintaining boundary-stones or other boundary marks, as well as the costs for the real conveyance of land and the necessary entries in the Ground Book are to be borne by the lessee or the purchaser.

The survey fees to be paid shall be calculated in accordance with the enclosed tariff (G).[1] Table I applies if the land has been surveyed and mapped (Section 36 of the Order regarding the Ground Book of 30th July 1887). Table II applies if the location and size of the land is only defined by a description and boundary marks on the site (Section 39 of the Order regarding the Ground Book of 30th July 1887).

Section 12

The Company takes no responsibility for the nature or the calculation of the size of land leased or sold, the calculated size, however, remains the basis for the implementation of the contract of lease or purchase, even if a later survey of the land shows variations.

---

1 This tariff (N.K.W.L., Vol. 4, 15) has not been translated.

Section 13

Rents are payable on 31st March of the current year for which they are due.

Section 14

If the lessee does not fulfil his financial obligations (Section 13) punctually, the Company is entitled to terminate the lease without notice. Thereupon the leased land reverts to the Company without compensation as it stands, that is with all buildings, crops and other installations erected or planted by the lessee.

The lessee can avert the consequences of the delay by paying within three months the amount due, plus a fine of one-twentieth of the rent due for each month until the payment is made.

The fine for parts of a month shall be calculated in proportion to the time elapsed.

Section 15

The rights arising out of a contract of lease can be transferred to third parties only with the approval of the Administrator or an authorised Station Manager.

Section 16

All precious stones, metals, in pure form or in ores, sulphur, coal, rock salt and other useful minerals, guano, phosphates, mineral oils, salt and other mineral springs as well as marble quarries which are located on or in land leased or sold shall be excluded from the lessee's or purchaser's right of disposal. The right to prospect for and exploit them is reserved exclusively to the Neu Guinea Kompagnie or persons authorised by it.

At any time lessees as well as owners are obliged to permit employees or persons authorised by the Neu Guinea Kompagnie to carry out inspections and tests for the purpose of locating such minerals, compensation being paid for any actual direct damage which may be caused to the surface of the land. The Neu Guinea Kompagnie is also entitled, at any time, to require in return for appropriate compensation, the return of such parts of a block of land which are, in the Administrator's estimation, considered necessary to prospect for, or to exploit the abovementioned minerals, as well as to transport the products,

Section 17

The Neu Guinea Kompagnie reserves to itself all rivers and streams which have been declared navigable, including a strip of land, 50 metres wide, along their banks as well as a strip of equal width (measured from the high-water mark) along the sea shore.

Lessees or owners of land adjoining such strips are allowed to use this land in return for a special payment, but with the proviso that this permission may be revoked at any time.

The use of other watercourses to drive any kind of machinery, likewise the erection of dams of any kind on such watercourses, as well as the diversion of water from them requires special permission. Lessees and owners of land on the banks of such watercourses must permit free of charge the floating of timber, as well as the use of the banks for this purpose as instructed by the Administration.

Section 18

Until this question has been regulated by law, the Neu Guinea Kompagnie reserves to itself the right to resume any land which, in the estimation of the Administrator, is required for roads, railways, canals, telegraph installations and other such public installations, compensation being paid to the lessee or owner for any actual direct damage.

It also reserves to itself the right to remove or to have removed by authorised persons at any time from land leased or sold, stones, clay, gravel, sand and other materials for the building or the maintenance of installations of the kind mentioned in the preceding Subsection, without payment for the material removed, but subject to compensation for any actual direct damage caused by the removal.

Section 19

Lessees and owners are bound by any instructions which the Administration may issue regarding the felling of trees in certain areas or of certain kinds of trees in the interests of the preservation of forests or of public health.

The lessee is not permitted to fell or destroy trees on his lease save for the erection of buildings on the land, for domestic use, or for the clearing of land which is to be cultivated forthwith. The extent to which this is permitted is subject to the approval of the Administration.

Section 20

If this has not been done already, the limitations and obligations set out in Sections 16 to 19 are to be entered in the Ground Book when ownership is transferred to the purchaser.

Section 21

When leased land reverts to the Company on expiry of the lease, an assessment will be made as to whether and to what extent the land has been improved by the erection of buildings, fences and other structures and what value these improvements possess. The Company shall have the choice of retaining the structures which are regarded as improvements on the land and paying the departing lessee their assessed value, or of allowing the entitled person to remove them.

Section 22

The final assessment of the compensation which is to be paid in cases covered by Section 16, Subsection 2 and Section 18, and the final assessment as to which of the structures at the reversion of a lease (Section 21)[1] are to be regarded as improvements and their value and also the extent to which their removal is to be permitted, shall be made by the Administrator after an inspection and valuation by experts, one of whom is appointed by each party.

Section 23

Settlers are bound by any regulations issued by the Administration regarding the employment of natives of the Protectorate as labourers, as well as regarding the supply of such labourers from the Company's labour depots.

Section 24

Each settler who enters into a contract of lease or purchase under these conditions, or his agent, is bound to provide the Station Manager of the district in which the block in question is situated with a postal address in the Protectorate to which the Administration of the Protectorate can serve all documents regarding the land with full effect – poste restante. If no such address is provided, the Administration is entitled to serve such documents – poste restante – to the post office of the district in which the block is situated.

Berlin, 15th February 1888

Neu Guinea Kompagnie
The Board of Directors

---

1 The German original says Section 20, but this is clearly a printing error.

IMPERIAL ORDINANCE REGARDING THE RIGHTS TO LAND IN THE GERMAN PROTECTORATES, OF 21st NOVEMBER 1902*

We, Wilhelm, by the Grace of God German Emperor, King of Prussia etc. order by virtue of Section 3 of the *Protectorates Act* (R.G.Bl., 1900, 813) in connection with Section 21 of the *Statute Regarding Consular Jurisdiction,* of 7th April 1900 (R.G.Bl., 1900, 213) for the German Protectorates in the name of the Reich as follows:

I. General Provisions

Section 1

The Civil laws regarding rights to land referred to in Section 19 of the *Statute Regarding Consular Jurisdiction* are applicable in accordance with Section 20, Subsection 1 of the said Statute, unless this Ordinance directs to the contrary.

The regulations which according to Sections 2 and 85 to 92 of the *Ground Book Act,* of 24th March 1897 (R.G.Bl., 1897, 139; 1898, 754) are to be issued by the local Sovereign, shall be issued by the Chancellor of the Reich or, with his approval, by the Governor.

Section 2

Sections 186, 189 of the *Statute Introducing the Civil Code,* Section 82 of the *Ground Book Act* and the *Prussian Ground Book Ordinance*, of 13th November 1899 (P.G. 1899, 519) are not applicable.

The laws referred to in Section 1, Subsection 1 apply to mining, compulsory auctions and sequestrations only in so far as the Chancellor of the Reich or, with his approval, the Governor declares them to be applicable.

The Chancellor of the Reich and, with his approval, the Governor can issue regulations regarding the acquisition, charging and termination of mining rights, as well as their relationship to other rights.

Section 3

The contemporaneous presence of both parties is not required for the transfer of land and it is also unnecessary for the same to make their declarations orally at the Ground Book Office.

---

1 D.K.G., Vol.6, 4-10.

Section 4

Amounts to be entered in the Ground Book can be stated in the currency of the Protectorate.

Section 5

The Chancellor of the Reich and, with his approval, the Governor shall determine the conditions for the acquisition of rights to ownerless and crown land. The relevant regulations in force at present in the individual Protectorates shall remain in force until they are repealed in accordance with the above provisions. No rights can be acquired contrary to existing regulations, or those to be issued.

Section 6

The following rules shall apply in respect of land belonging to natives or other coloured persons:

1) If and in so far as appears necessary in the public interest the Chancellor of the Reich and, with his approval, the Governor are authorised to either prohibit the acquisition of ownership or other real rights to such land and also its use by third parties, or to make it subject to special conditions or administrative approval. The same applies to the acquisition and the charging of such land by way of compulsory auction. Section 5, Sentences 2 and 3 are correspondingly applicable.
2) Otherwise this Ordinance only applies to such land if a folio in the Ground Book has been established for it, or if it has been entered into a Land Register (Section 19). To what extent natives or other coloured persons are entitled or can be requested to have their land registered in the Ground Book shall be determined by the Chancellor of the Reich and, with his approval, by the Governor.
3) The Chancellor of the Reich and, with his approval, the Governor can direct in favour of natives or other coloured persons:
    a) that forms for the charging of such land other than those contained in the Third Book of the *Civil Code* and Section 40 of the *Prussian Statute Implementing the Civil Code,* shall be admissible,
    b) that Ground Book folios can be established for certain rights of usufruct, even if they are not inheritable or are non-transferable, and that the law regarding land belonging to natives shall continue to apply to them.

II. The Establishing of New Ground Book Folios

Section 7

Ground Book folios can be established only if a parish map already exists, or if the survey of the land and the drawing of a map are practicable. The conditions under which a survey is to be regarded as practicable are to be determined by the Chancellor of the Reich. He can also permit the establishing of folios in individual cases, if a survey in the sense of this Section is not practicable, or if the cost connected with it would be out of proportion to the value of the land.

Section 8

A Ground Book folio shall be established upon application of the owner, or of a person who can demand an entry in the Ground Book by virtue of an executable order against the owner, in so far as this entry must be preceded by the entry of the owner.

The Chancellor of the Reich and, with his approval, the Governor can prescribe that the owner be requested *ex officio* to make the application (Sub-section 1) and in what manner, and with what effect. The relevant regulations which are in force at present in the individual Protectorates shall remain in force until they are repealed in accordance with the above provision.

Section 9

Together with the application the applicant must, by means of documents, attestations by public authorities or in any other way, establish a *prima facie* case that he has acquired the land as owner, or that he has been in undisturbed possession of it.

The land which is to be registered must be described in the application with regard to location and boundaries, any special name and other distinguishing marks and, if possible, with regard to cultivation or manner of use and size.

A map showing the land must accompany the application. This does not affect Section 7, Sentence 3.

Section 10

The establishing of a Ground Book folio must be preceded by a public notice.

Section 11

The public notice shall be issued by the Ground Book Office. It must contain:

1. The name of the applicant,
2. a description of the land in question, and
3. an invitation to all those who claim ownership of the land, or another

right suitable for registration to assert their rights and claims and to provide before a certain date *prima facie* evidence of these, failing which the folio will be established without regard for their rights and claims.

The notice is to be displayed on the public notice board and to be made public in any other suitable way.

The first publication of the notice and the date set for the hearing must be separated by a period of at least three months.

Section 12

If, before the set date, no other claim to ownership has been lodged or if it has not been supported by *prima facie* evidence, the folio will be established. The Ground Book Office is also entitled *ex officio* to take into account *prima facie* claims of third parties which have come to its notice. In the case of contradictory claims the folio can be established only after the parties involved have settled their claims.

Section 13

Rights which have been brought to notice before the set date (Section 11, No. 3) are to be entered in the folio when it is established, if the applicant acknowledges the right claimed or if the conditions exist for an entry as laid down in this Ordinance.

Otherwise an objection will be entered as a safeguard for the right claimed, provided a *prima facie* case has been established for its existence.

If the parties involved cannot reach agreement, the precedence of the rights which have been brought to notice before the set date shall be determined by legal action.

Section 14

The Ground Book Office can establish a folio in the Ground Book without issuing a public notice:

1. If the application for the registration of the land is based on a transfer of previously ownerless land and if the transfer and the occupation took place by virtue of a contract with the Treasury or a permit from the Government,
2. if the application for the establishing of a folio is made in accordance with Section 8 by a person whose claim has been found to be legally valid in accordance with one of the following regulations:
   a) in the Pacific Protectorates, with the exception of Samoa, in accordance with No. IV of the *Declaration Relating to the Reciprocal Freedom of Trade and Commerce in the German and British Possessions and Protectorates in the Western Pacific*, of 10th April 1886,

b) in German New Guinea in accordance with Sections 6 to 11 of the *Ordinance Regarding the Acquisition of Ownership and the Charging of Land in the Protectorate of the Neu Guinea Kompagnie,* of 20th July 1887 (R.G.Bl., 1887, 379),

c) in Samoa in accordance with Section IV of the *General Act of the Samoa Conference in Berlin,* of 14th June 1889,

d) in the Protectorate of the Marshall Islands in accordance with Sections 6 and 7 of the *Ordinance Regarding the Acquisition of Ownership and the Charging of Land in the Protectorate of the Marshall Islands,* of 22nd June 1889 (R.G.Bl., 1889, 145),

e) in German South-West Africa in accordance with the *Ordinance Regarding Mining in the South-West African Protectorate,* of 6th September 1892 (R.G.Bl., 1892, 789) and the *Ordinance Regarding Public Notice Proceedings for Land Claims in the South-West African Protectorate,* of 2nd April 1893 (R.G.Bl., 1893, 143),

f) in the Island Territory of the Carolines, Palaus and Marianas in accordance with Section 13 of the *Ordinance Regarding the Preliminary Regulation of the Administration and the Legal Conditions in the Island Territory of the Carolines, Palaus and Marianas,* of 26th September 1899.

Section 15

In the case of Section 14 all those who claim to have rights to the land suitable for registration in the Ground Book shall be summoned after the folio has been established to assert and to provide *prima facie* evidence for their rights by a certain date, failing which these rights shall be disregarded if other applications for registration are made. Section 11, Subsections 2 and 3 and Section 12 are correspondingly applicable.

The Chancellor of the Reich and, with his approval, the Governor can determine whether and under what conditions Subsection 1 shall not be applied.

Section 16

Sections 14 and 15 are also applicable if the applicant has acquired claims based on the transfer of previously ownerless land, or if claims which have already been found to be legally valid have been acquired by the applicant by way of succession of title.

Section 17

Section 8, Section 9, Subsection 1, and Sections 10 to 16 are not applicable in the Protectorate of Kiautschou. Instead the following provisions shall apply there:

A Ground Book folio for land shall be established for either the Treasury, on application of the competent public authority, or for the person who has acquired the land from the Treasury. A written declaration from the Governor, that the Treasury has acquired ownership, shall be necessary and sufficient to establish the Treasury as the owner of the land in relation to the Ground Book Office.

The transfer of land belonging to the Treasury, which has not yet been registered, does not have to be preceded by the establishing of a Ground Book folio.

III. Provisions regarding Land for which a Ground Book Folio has not yet been Established

Section 18

The laws referred to in Section 1, Subsection 1 which deal with the transfer of ownership of land do not apply to land for which a Ground Book folio has not been established.

To transfer the ownership of such land, agreement between the transferor and the transferee shall be necessary and sufficient. The declarations must be made in a publicly attested form. An attestation by a public authority in the Protectorate is sufficient.

The transfer of ownership cannot be made subject to any conditions or to any stipulation as to time.

Section 19

The owner can have his ownership entered in a Land Register to be kept by the competent Ground Book Office. A person who can apply for the establishing of a Ground Book folio by virtue of an executable order against the owner (Section 8, Subsection 1) has the same right. Section 8, Subsection 2 is correspondingly applicable.

Section 20

Upon application for the registration of ownership it must be proved that ownership has been acquired.

The land in question must be described as exactly as possible. The Ground Book Office shall decide whether or not the description is sufficiently exact.

Section 21

If someone is entered in the Land Register as the owner of land it will be presumed that he is the owner.

Section 22

Land of the kind defined in Section 18, Subsection 1 cannot be encumbered with any rights other than hypothecs or land charges.

With regard to hypothecs or land charges entry in the Land Register shall have the same effect as an entry in the Ground Book. However, even with regard to hypothecs or land charges the Land Register does not have the effect that third parties can rely on the registered owner being the true owner of the land.

Section 23

A hypothec or land charge can only be registered in such a way that the issuing of a certificate of charge is excluded.

Section 24

Sections 18 to 23 are not applicable in the Protectorate of Kiautschou.

IV. Final Provisions

Section 25

Ownership of land which belongs to the Reich by virtue of statutory provisions, in particular Section 1 of the *Ordinance Regarding the Creation, Occupation and Transfer of Crown Land and the Acquisition and Transfer of Land in German East Africa,* of 26th November 1895, and Section 1 of the *Ordinance Regarding the Creation, Occupation and Transfer of Crown Land and the Acquisition and Transfer of Land in the Protectorate of the Cameroons,* of 15th June 1896, or by virtue of contractual agreements before the proclamation of this Ordinance, shall be deemed to have been acquired by the Treasury of the Protectorate in which the land in question is situated. The same applies with regard to real rights to land.

Subsection 1 does not apply to land used for naval and postal purposes and to land situated in the Protectorate of the Marshall Islands.

Section 26

The Chancellor of the Reich and, with his approval, the Governor are to issue the orders necessary to implement this Ordinance, especially regarding the establishing and the keeping of Ground Books and Land Registers.

Section 27

The duties assigned to the Chancellor of the Reich in this Ordinance shall be fulfilled on his behalf by the Foreign Office (Colonial Section) for the Protectorates in Africa and the Pacific and by the Naval Office of the Reich for the Protectorate of Kiautschou.

The term 'Governor', as used in this Ordinance, also includes the Administrator of the Protectorate of the Marshall Islands and the Vice-Governor of the Island Territory of the Carolines, Palaus and Marianas.

Section 28

This Ordinance shall come into force on 1st April 1903. At the same time the following laws shall become ineffective, in so far as Sections 5, 6, 8 and 14 do not direct to the contrary:

1. The *Ordinance Regarding the Acquisition of Ownership and the Charging of Land in the Protectorate of the Neu Guinea Kompagnie,* of 20th July 1887 (R.G.Bl., 1887, 379),
2. the *Ordinance Regarding the Acquisition of Ownership and the Charging of Land in the Protectorate of the Marshall Islands,* of 22nd June 1889 (R.G.Bl., 1889, 145),
3. the *Ordinance Regarding the Establishing of Rights of Pledge to Land In German East-Africa,* of 18th March 1892,
4. the *Ordinance Regarding the Registration of Land Titles in Samoa,* of 19th January 1894,
5. the *Ordinance Regarding the Legal Conditions of Immovable Property in German East-Africa,* of 24th July 1894,
6. the *Ordinance Regarding the Regulation of the Acquisition of Land in Kiautschou,* of 2nd September 1898,
7. the *Ordinance Regarding the Legal Conditions of Immovable Property in German South-West Africa,* of 5th October 1898 (R.G.Bl., 1898, 1063),
8. Section 3, Sentence 1 of the *Ordinance Regarding the Legal Conditions in the German Protectorates,* of 9th November 1900 (R.G.Bl., 1900, 1005),
9. the *Ordinance Regarding the Legal Conditions of Land in the Cameroons,* of 24th June 1901,
10. the *Ordinance Regarding the Legal Conditions of Land in Togo,* of 5th November 1901,
11. the Orders issued in implementation of the Ordinances named in Nos. 1 to 7, 9 and 10.

Executed with our own hand and under the Imperial Seal.
Given on board M.Y. *Hohenzollern,* Helgoland, 21st November 1902.

(L.S.)

Wilhelm I.R.
Graf v. Bülow

ORDER BY THE GOVERNOR OF GERMAN NEW GUINEA FOR THE PROTECTORATE OF GERMAN NEW GUINEA, EXCLUDING THE ISLAND TERRITORY OF THE CAROLINES, PALAUS AND MARIANAS, IN IMPLEMENTATION OF THE IMPERIAL ORDINANCE REGARDING THE RIGHTS TO LAND IN THE GERMAN PROTECTORATES, OF 21st NOVEMBER 1902 AND THE ORDER ISSUED THERETO BY THE CHANCELLOR OF THE REICH ON 30th NOVEMBER 1902, OF 22nd JULY 1904*

By virtue of Sections 1 and 26 of the *Imperial Ordinance Regarding the Rights to Land in the German Protectorates,* of 21st November 1902 (R.G.Bl., 1900, 283) and with the approval of the Chancellor of the Reich, I hereby order for the Protectorate of German New Guinea, excluding the Island Territory of the Carolines, Palaus and Marianas, as follows:

Section 1

(to Section 1, Subsection 2 of the Imperial Ordinance)

The official list (Section 2, Subsection 2 of the *Ground Book Act*) shall be kept separately for each Ground Book district by the competent Ground Book Office in accordance with the attached example.

Each block of land shall be given a separate page. Amendments must be entered in the relevant column below the original entry. Entries which are no longer valid must be underlined in red ink.

Section 2

(to Section 2, Subsection 2 of the Imperial Ordinance)

The laws referred to in Section 1, Subsection 1 of the Imperial Ordinance are applicable to compulsory auctions and sequestrations as soon as the land has been entered in the Ground Book or Land Register.

The compulsory auction and sequestration of land which has not yet been entered in the Ground Book or Land Register are governed by the provisions in Part 4 of the Prussian *Statute Regarding the Execution into Immovable Property,* of 13th July 1883 (P.G., 1883, 131), intended for the area in which the *Prussian Common Law* has hitherto applied, with the proviso that in so far as they refer to provisions made elsewhere in the same Statute, these

* D.K.G., Vol.8, 157-161.

provisions shall be replaced by the corresponding provisions contained in the laws which, according to Subsection 1, apply to land entered in the Ground Book or the Land Register.

Section 3

(to Sections 5 and 6 of the Imperial Ordinance)

1. The right to occupy and to dispose of ownerless land as well as the right to conclude contracts with the natives regarding the acquisition of ownership or real rights to land or the use thereof shall be exclusively held by the Treasury which can be represented in any relevant legal actions by persons other than officials at the discretion of the Governor. Land required by the natives for their sustenance, in particular dwelling places, garden land and palm groves, is excluded from acquisition.
2. The deed to be drawn up when ownerless land is occupied, must show how the 'appropriation' took place, contain a precise description of the boundaries and state the manner in which the given boundary points have been marked.

   At his discretion the Governor shall issue further directions regarding the contents of the contracts with the natives and of the contracts regarding the re-transfer of land which the Treasury has acquired from natives or occupied as ownerless, either generally by drawing up appropriate contract forms, or from case to case.
3. To what extent natives are entitled or can be requested to enter their land in the Ground Book or the Land Register shall be determined in each individual case by the Governor.
4. The *Directions Regarding the Procedures for the Acquisition of Land by the Neu Guinea Kompagnie,* of 10th August 1887 as well as the supplements issued thereto for the District of Northern New Ireland on 24th January 1902 and for Kaiser Wilhelmsland on 28th July 1903 are repealed.

Section 4

(to Section 8, Subsection 2 of the Imperial Ordinance)

1. The Ground Book Office can enjoin land owners to apply for registration in the Ground Book by means of fines, the total of which may not exceed 300 marks.

   If an application is not made within three months, to be reckoned from the date of the first summons, the Ground Book Office can *ex officio* order the registration and a survey of the land, in so far as this is necessary. Costs and expenses incurred in this case must be borne by the owner.

2. Persons for whom rights to land in the Protectorate are to be entered in the Ground Book, but who are neither residents of the Protectorate nor live there permanently, must, at the request of the Ground Book Office, appoint and name to the Ground Book Office a representative in the Protectorate to deal with all matters relating to the establishing of a Ground Book folio. The same applies to companies who are not incorporated in the Protectorate. The fulfilment of this obligation can be enforced by means of administrative fines of up to 100 marks. If, notwithstanding the levying of an administrative fine, no representative is appointed within the period of time stipulated for the party, the Ground Book Office can appoint a representative *ex officio*.
3. Objections to orders under Nos. 1 and 2 can be lodged in accordance with the provisions applying to Ground Book matters.

Section 5

(to Section 15, Subsection 2 of the Imperial Ordinance)

In cases of Section 14, No. 1 of the Imperial Ordinance, Section 15, Subsection 1 of the said Ordinance is not to be applied.

Section 6

(to Section 26 of the Imperial Ordinance in connection with Section 2, Subsection 1 and Section 3, Subsection 2 of the Order of the Chancellor of the Reich)

1. The hitherto existing Ground Book districts shall remain.
2. The Ground Books kept hitherto in the 13 Ground Book districts shall be deemed to be Ground Books. These are:
   in the jurisdiction of the Court in Herbertshöhe:
   a) the Gazelle Peninsula and the smaller and adjacent islands; the southern boundary follows a straight line from the mouth of the Toriu River to the mouth of the Reed River;
   b) New Britain and the smaller adjacent islands, excluding the Gazelle Peninsula;
   c) the Duke of York Islands;
   d) New Ireland I, comprising the north-western half from the Steffen Strait to the 152nd degree of east longitude, and the smaller adjacent islands, including Simberi, Tabar and Napakur (Fischer and Gardner Islands);
   e) New Ireland II, comprising the south-eastern half from the 152nd degree of east longitude, Lihir Island (Gerrit-Denys-Island) and the smaller adjacent islands to the north and east thereof as far as the 155th degree of east longitude;

f) New Hanover from the Steffen Strait onward and the surrounding islands as well as the islands of Mussau (St. Matthias), Squally and Portland;

g) the Manus Group (Admiralty Islands) and the surrounding islands between the Equator and the 3rd degree of south latitude and between the 142nd and 149th degrees of east longitude;

h) the German Solomon Islands and the small islands to the north thereof;

in the jurisdiction of the Court in Friedrich Wilhelmshafen:

i) Berlinhafen, from the Dutch border to the Sepik River, including the adjacent islands;

k) Hatzfeldthafen, from the Sepik River to Cape Croisilles, including the adjacent islands;

l) Friedrich Wilhelmshafen, from Cape Croisilles to the Gogol River, including the adjacent islands;

m) Constantinhafen, from the Gogol River to the 147th degree of east longitude, including the adjacent islands;

n) Finschhafen, from the 147th degree of east longitude to the British border, including the adjacent islands as well as the French Islands, Long Island and Umboi (Rook Island), and the islands adjacent to the last two islands.

The date for the establishment of the Ground Book shall be the 1st July 1905, unless the Ground Book has already been established for individual Ground Books districts in accordance with previous orders.

3. The form hitherto used shall continue to be used with the following amendments:

   a) the head of the title page shall read: 'Ground Book of the Protectorate of German New Guinea'
   Volume . . . .
   Folio No. . . . .

   b) in the first column of the title page, the number which the individual component part bears in the official list (Section 1) is to be added in brackets under its number.

   c) In the third column of the third section 'hypothecs, land charges and annuity charges' is to be substituted for 'hypothecs'.

4. The Land Registers are to be kept separately for each Ground Book district. The entries and documents relating to a block of land shall form a separate register file. The files shall be numbered in running order.

Section 7

This Order shall come into force on 1st July 1905.

Herbertshöhe, 22nd July 1904

The Imperial Governor
Hahl

Enclosure

Protectorate of German New Guinea

Official List

of the blocks of land in the Ground Book district of . . . .

Number . . . .

Name (description) of the block of land . . . .

Number . . . . Volume . . . . of the Ground Book

1	2	3	4
Short description of the location according to district and boundaries	Area[1]	Owner	Remarks

[1] In hectares, ares and square metres. (One are equals 100 square metres).

GENERAL CONDITIONS FOR THE TRANSFER OF LAND BY THE TREASURY OF GERMAN NEW GUINEA, 1904 – 1910*

I

If the Treasury sells land which has been surveyed in accordance with the *Principles Regarding the Survey of Land outside an Established Trigonometrical Grid* (Enclosure I to the Order by the Chancellor of the Reich of 30th November 1902), the Governor will retain the right to order a more precise determination of the boundaries of the survey.

If this survey shows that the area is smaller than assumed at the time of the sale, the purchase price is to be reduced accordingly, unless agreement is reached that the purchaser is to be assigned other land to make up the deficiency; the purchaser has however no claim to be assigned such land elsewhere.

The deficiency in area entitles the purchaser only to a reduction in the purchase price, as stipulated in the preceding Subsection.

II

The purchaser shall bear the cost of acquiring the land by contract with the natives or of occupying ownerless land, of surveying and demarcating it, and of entering it in the Ground Book and Land Register, as well as the cost of inspecting the land, if this is deemed necessary by the Administration or the Ground Book Judge.

III

Duly acquired rights of third parties to the land sold shall be protected. The Treasury does not guarantee that the land sold is not subject to rights of third parties.

IV

The purchaser is bound to commence operations on the land within two years, unless prevented by circumstances for which he is not responsible. Failing this he must retransfer to the Treasury the ownership granted to him.

---

*

These General Conditions were not published in any of the collections of German Colonial laws. A photocopy of the original on which this translation is based has been deposited in the Library of the Supreme Court of Papua New Guinea.

The purchaser is further under obligation to invest within fifteen years at least fifteen marks per hectare on at least three-quarters of the land. The money can be spent on cultivating the land, on preparing it for grazing or forestry, in particular on procuring breeding stock, and on erecting buildings of lasting value. The costs listed in Section II shall not count towards the necessary investments.

If the purchaser does not prove during the first half of the sixteenth year at the latest that he has fulfilled the obligations stipulated above, or that he has been prevented from fulfilling them by circumstances for which he is not responsible, he must retransfer to the Treasury the whole area of land for which, according to the books, the minimum investment has not been made.

The periods of time stipulated in this Section commence on the first day of the calendar quarter following the execution of the contract.

V

Any precious stones, metals (in pure form or in ores), sulphur, coal, rock salt and other useful minerals, guano, phosphate, mineral oils, salt and other mineral springs, as well as marble quarries which are located on or in the land sold are excluded from the purchaser's right of disposal. The right to prospect for and exploit them is reserved exclusively to the Treasury or to a person authorised by the Governor, in so far as the conditions under which mining can be carried out have not been specifically regulated by way of statute, decree or concession.

At any time the purchaser is obliged to permit officials or persons authorised by the Governor to carry out inspections and tests for the purpose of locating such minerals, compensation being paid for any actual direct damage which may be caused to the surface of the land.

The Governor is also entitled, at any time, to require in return for appropriate compensation, the return of such parts of the land sold, which are in the Governor's estimation, considered necessary to prospect for,[1] or to exploit the abovementioned minerals, as well as to transport the products.

VI

The purchaser is obliged to sell to the Treasury at cost price land required for roads, railways and telegraph installations, landing-places and other public installations.

---

*

The German original says *Unternehmung* instead of *Untersuchung*, but a a comparison with Section 16 of the 1888 Conditions (see above, p.32), from which this paragraph is taken, clearly show that this is an error.

If the clearing or cultivating of land resumed under this provision has already begun, the cost of clearing or cultivating is in every case also to be refunded, in so far as satisfactory evidence can be produced.

Amendment

Herbertshöhe, 14th February 1907

1.

The purchaser can be required by the Ground Book Judge to have the land surveyed at his own expense by a certified surveyor:

a) if for some reason such a surveyor comes to the area in question and if the re-survey can be carried out without undue difficulty and expense,
b) if another person acquires ownership of land adjoining the first block.

2.

The owner of the land must accept as final any later determination of the boundaries by a certified surveyor and has no claim against the Treasury or the adjoining owner if the size of his block is altered.

3.

He has no claim for damages against the Treasury for any errors in the original survey and is liable to the Treasury, if claims are made against it by third parties because of such errors.

It will be necessary to establish and to enter in the Ground Book a cautionary hypothec to secure the fulfilment of this obligation only if this has been expressly stated by me in the authorisation to acquire land for the Treasury.

The Imperial Governor
(signed) Hahl

Amendment II

Rabaul, 3rd March 1910

Without any claim to compensation, the purchaser (lessee) is obliged: to suffer the drainage of rainwater from public roads onto and across his land, to maintain public roads which touch or traverse his land, and in particular to keep them free of trees and the grass short, irrespective of who owns the road.

This obligation does not exist for those roads and paths for whose maintenance the Treasury has specifically accepted or will accept responsibility.

The Imperial Governor
(signed) Hahl

FORM FOR THE AUTHORISATION OF PRIVATE INDIVIDUALS TO ACQUIRE LAND FOR THE TREASURY OF GERMAN NEW GUINEA, OF ABOUT 1904*

To . . . .
Following your application I authorise you under the following conditions to acquire . . . hectares of land in the district . . . for the Treasury of German New Guinea, either by contract with the natives or by the occupation of ownerless land.

1. The land is to be sold to you under the *General Conditions for the Transfer of Land by the Treasury of German New Guinea* stipulated by me . . . and under special conditions which still have to be negotiated. Should I for any reason later not be in a position to transfer to you the land you have acquired for the Treasury, you shall have no claim to be reimbursed for your expenses (travelling expenses, purchase price paid to the natives etc.).
2. You are not permitted to acquire land which is used by the natives to gain their livelihood and such land will under no circumstances be re-sold to you.
3. On an average the river- or sea-frontage per each . . . square metre(s) may not be more than 1 metre. The boundaries must run inland from the sea shore or river banks at an angle which is as close to 90 degrees as possible.
4. If the land is sold to you by the Treasury you are to pay a purchase price of . . . marks per hectare. Your expenses (travel expenses, purchase price paid to the natives etc.) do not count towards this purchase price.
5. You are to bear the cost of the survey.
6. This authority will become invalid if the land is not selected within one year.

---

* This form was not published in any of the collections of German Colonial law. A photocopy of the original on which this translation is based has been deposited in the library of the Supreme Court of Papua New Guinea.

FORM FOR THE PURCHASE OF LAND FOR THE TREASURY OF GERMAN NEW GUINEA, OF ABOUT 1904*

. . . , . . . 19 . . .

The undersigned . . . has been authorised by the Imperial Governor to acquire land. The original (copy) of the authority is attached. He went today to the actual location in order to acquire from the natives the land which is shown on the map attached to this contract.

First of all the undersigned together with the also undersigned . . . as interpreter and . . . as witness(es) carried out the following investigations by questioning the following natives.

I. Natives Questioned

(Name) (Estimated age) (Place of residence)

1. . . . .

10. . . . .

II. Investigations

1. Who is, in the opinion of the natives involved, entitled to decide about the permanent transfer of the land?

   . . . .

2. What procedures for such a transfer are customary among them and have to be followed in order to make the transfer valid?

   . . . .

3. To which persons must the purchase price be paid to release the purchaser effectively from his contractual obligations?

   . . . .

4. Will the natives living in the vicinity retain sufficient land after the sale of the land in question to gain their livelihood? . . . .
   (Total area of the land in the possession of the natives involved) . . . .
   (Size of the land to be sold) . . . .
   (Number of men, women and children) . . . .

---

* This form was not published in any of the collections of German Colonial law. A photocopy of the original on which this translation is based has been deposited in the library of the Supreme Court of Papua New Guinea.

5. What roads and market places exist?

. . . .

6. What fishing rights exist?

. . . .

Hereupon the boundaries of the land to be acquired were established, in accordance with the *Principles for the Survey of Land outside an Established Trigonometrical Grid*, in the presence of all the natives who, according to these investigations, have interests in the land and with the assistance of the interpreter and witness. Thereupon 2 copies of a map corresponding to these Principles were made.

Presently 2 identical copies of the following contract with the native right-holders were recorded in the German language.

One copy of the contract and the map was handed over to the vendor . . . .

(signature of the purchaser) . . . .

(signature of the interpreter) . . . .

(signature of the witness) . . . .

Contract

Between

1. the Treasury of the Protectorate of German New Guinea represented by the Imperial Governor, the latter represented by . . .

purchaser

and

2. the natives of the village – district . . .

Names:

1. . . . .

.

.

10. . . . .

vendors.

With the assistance of . . . and the participation of . . . as interpreter of the language familiar to the vendors and . . . as witness, the following contract of purchase and sale has been made on this . . . day of . . ., 19 . . . .

Clause 1

The persons named under 2. sell and transfer to the Treasury the ownership of the land called . . . .

It is located as follows . . . .

Area about . . . hectares

Type . . . .
Boundaries to
the north . . . .
the east . . . .
the south . . . .
the west . . . .

A map of the land is attached to this contract. Existing roads and market places as well as existing fishing rights are not included in the sale; the latter shall be entered in the Ground Book.

The purchase price is . . . marks which are to be paid in cash (goods). The price at which the individual goods have been charged to the vendors is shown in Clause 2.

The vendors affirm that the land sold has hitherto been their exclusive property, that they also hold the exclusive right to dispose of it and that they alone are entitled to receive the agreed purchase price.

It has been made clear to them and understood by them that, by transferring the land and accepting the purchase price for it, they renounce all claims to it for themselves and their families for all times, so that they can neither take it into possession nor sell it again, but that, on the contrary, only the purchaser will henceforth be entitled to use and dispose of it, and that the purchaser will in future have the exclusive right to dispose of coconuts and other tree crops growing on the land.

Clause 2

In accordance with the agreement reached the purchase price has been handed over to the vendors; it has been distributed as follows:

(cash:) (goods:)

1. . . . .
.
.
10. . . . .

The same acknowledge receipt and declare that all their claims have thereby been satisfied.

Conversely the block of land has been delivered and the representative of the Treasury affirms for his part that the delivery has taken place.

In witness thereof the above contract has been executed by both parties as follows, by the vendors, after it was made clear to them that they thereby make their consent final and binding.

(Signature of the purchaser) . . . .
(Signature or mark of the vendors) . . . .

In addition to the vendors their assistants have, after the same explanation, affixed their signature (mark) below:

. . . .

That the proceedings have been correctly translated into the . . . language with which the vendors are familiar is confirmed by:
(Signature of the interpreter) . . . .
Present as witness during the proceedings and certifying his conviction that the transferors have been made aware of the significance of the transfer:
(Signature of the witness) . . . .

PRINCIPLES FOR THE TRANSFER OF LAND IN THE PROTECTORATE OF NEW GUINEA, INCLUDING THE ISLAND TERRITORY, OF 24th APRIL 1912*

I

Exclusive right of the Treasury to acquire land etc.[1]

The acquisition of land or real rights to land by occupying ownerless land or by contracts with the natives shall be reserved to the Treasury.

As a matter of principle no contracts between non-natives or non-indigenous natives and natives of the Protectorate regarding the acquisition of land or real rights to land shall be ratified. Nor shall, as a rule, contracts with natives be ratified which concern the use of native land in any other form.

In administratively organised areas, the acquisition of land for the Treasury by occupying ownerless land or by contracts with natives is to be carried out by an official of the Protectorate. Other persons can also be authorised by being given a special written authority (Form A) to acquire land for the Treasury outside administratively organised areas, and also within them, if the acquisition by an official is impracticable, due to circumstances. The authority cannot be transferred, pledged, sold or inherited. Land so acquired shall later be transferred to the acquirer by way of sale or lease, but the authority does not establish a legal claim to the transfer. Incidental expenses shall not be refunded to the authorised person, even if the land is not subsequently transferred; the question of possible refunds by the natives solely concerns the Treasury.

Before land is bought from the natives, or occupied as ownerless, the competent local administration official (District Commissioner or District Officer) is to be given an opportunity to comment upon the selection of the land. The acquisition documents are to be handed to the competent administration official for submission to the Government. If the land has not

* These Principles were not published in any of the collections of German Colonial laws. A photocopy of the original on which this translation is based has been deposited in the library of the Supreme Court of Papua New Guinea.

1 This and all following 'headings', printed in this way, appear in the margin in the original German document. To avoid an excessively wide margin they have been incorporated in the text.

been selected and the acquisition documents have not been handed in within a year from the date of issue of the authority, the latter will become ineffective with the expiry of that year.

A person who cultivates, builds or plants on land bought from natives or occupied as ownerless without the consent of the Government, shall not acquire any rights thereby. He shall be obliged to leave the land without compensation.

II

Principles regarding the land to be transferred

A.

The following types of land are on principle excluded from transfer to private ownership:

1. Land which is used by the public, e.g. public roads, public landing-places, public wells, market places, springs, navigable rivers, etc.
2. Land which is inhabited by natives or has been taken into agricultural use by them, land which natives require to construct and house their sea-craft and fishing-tackle (taking into account that it must also remain possible for the natives to use boats and cutters as sea-craft), uninhabited small islands which the natives use as resting places while fishing, and land which has been set aside as a native reserve. The area of the land intended for a native reserve will depend on the actual local conditions.
3. Land in the vicinity of government posts and of built-up areas.
4. Coastal land in the vicinity of important harbours and landing places, as well as at the mouth of navigable rivers.
5. Whole islands or groups of islands.
6. Small blocks of land which, on account of their location and size, are suitable only for the erection of trading stations without plantations directly attached.
7. Land which in its original state, that is without being cleared and cultivated, already yields a sufficient quantity of produce to warrant permanent management. This will depend on whether the useful plants already there can produce, in the long term, sufficient returns to cover, from the outset, a substantial part of the costs of proper management and of increasing the returns in the future.

   A lease or the right to use land of the type described above shall be granted under specially stipulated conditions.
8. Land which is more suited to forestry than to agricultural use. The Protectorate's stocks of useful and fine timbers not situated on private property shall be exploited by the granting of temporary timber cutting

rights which shall be restricted in accordance with the principles of forestry.

9. The sea shore, which remains the property of the Government, and adjacent reefs.

B.

1. Each block of land which is to be transferred shall, as far as possible, be rectangular, unless the coastline, river banks and roads suggest that another shape is more suitable, or unless this is necessitated by natural boundaries. In particular it shall be inadmissible to exclude land from a block, simply because it is of inferior quality (see IV, No. 3). In the case of larger land acquisitions continuous blocks are to be selected wherever possible. If, for special reasons, land is acquired in several places, each block shall comprise at least 500 hectares.
As a rule no block of land shall extend along the shore, the banks of a navigable river, or a public road suitable for vehicles for more than two-thirds of its average depth, each side of a river or road being treated separately.

2. Insofar as certain protective provisions for the preservation of the forest appear to be necessary on account of the natural topography, the right is reserved to impose special regulations in individual cases. The same will apply should it become necessary to regulate the rights to running water.

III

Principles regarding the person of the acquirer

1. As a rule government land shall not be transferred into the ownership of natives or persons who do not have the status of Europeans.
2. Persons other than those defined in No. 1 are in principle excluded from buying or leasing government land, if they are not able to read and write a European language.
3. Government land shall not be transferred to subjects of states where the acquisition of land by citizens of the Reich is restricted, or shall be transferred only under corresponding restrictions.
4. Companies and legal persons are allowed to acquire government land only if they have been incorporated in accordance with German law in Germany or a German Protectorate.
5. In all but exceptional cases, additional land shall be transferred to companies or legal persons who have already more than 2000 hectares in their possession, only if they have cultivated three-quarters of their holdings.
As a rule no further land shall be transferred to companies who have more than 5000 hectares in their possession.

The same applies to individuals, but in their case the relevant areas are half of those defined above.

The stipulated limitations may be exceeded, if this is made necessary by the type of cultivation or utilisation intended.

6. The other restrictions on legal persons are governed by the existing laws (Pr.A.G.B.G.B., S.6, S.7).
7. Any person who acquires or possesses the right to use land in the Protectorate, be it as owner, lessee or in any other form must, if he does not reside in the Protectorate or if he leaves it for more than six months, name a resident European as a representative of his interests to the authorities.

   Declarations by the authorities, notices etc., shall be deemed to have been served on the rightholder as soon as they have been served on his representative.

   If no nomination is made, all documents affecting the land are deemed to have been served as soon as they have been displayed for one month on the notice board of the competent local administrative authority.
8. The purchaser must show that he possesses a working capital of 20,000 marks for every 100 hectares he wishes to acquire.
9. The existing special conditions shall continue to apply to the acquisition of land by missions. The re-transfer of land transferred to missions is permissible only with the approval of the Government. The Government can demand that this restriction be entered into the Ground Book.

IV

General conditions for the sale of land (Form B)

Government land shall be sold under the following conditions:

1. No guarantee is given that the land is of the size assumed at the sale, even if it has been surveyed. If the land was not surveyed at the time of the sale, the purchaser is under obligation to have the land surveyed later by a certified surveyor at his own expense, if he is requested to do so. The owner of the land must accept as final any subsequent determination of the boundaries by a certified surveyor and has no claim against either the Treasury or the adjoining owner if the size of his block is altered.

   He has no claim for damages against the Treasury for any errors in the original survey.

   On request, the purchaser must establish a cautionary hypothec to secure the fulfilment of the above obligation.
2. Duly acquired rights by third parties to the land sold are protected.

The Treasury does not guarantee that the land sold is not subject to rights of third parties.

3. The purchase price shall be determined according to the location of the land, the type of soil and its intended use and at present amounts, as a rule, to 5 marks per hectare, or portions thereof. No guarantee whatsoever is given that the selected land is suitable for the purpose for which the acquirer intends to use it. If blocks of land, following the principle laid down in II, B, No. 1, include substantial areas which are clearly not suitable for any economic use, a lower uniform price can be fixed for certain portions.
After the contract of purchase and sale has been executed, no reduction of the purchase price is possible.
4. If unsurveyed land is sold and a certain area is stated, the purchase price will be correspondingly reduced, or increased, if the subsequent survey shows that the land falls short of, or exceeds the area assumed at the sale. If the area is deficient, the Government is entitled to assign other land to the purchaser to make up the deficiency, instead of refunding part of the purchase price. The purchaser has however no claim to be assigned such land.
5. The purchaser shall bear the cost of acquiring the land by contract with the natives or of occupying ownerless land and supply the necessary labour and services for the boundaries to be preliminarily fixed; he also bears the cost of the survey and demarcation, even if they take place before the transfer of ownership, as well as the costs of the real conveyance and entry in the Ground Book. These incidental expenses must be paid at once, with the exception of the cost of the survey for which respite of payment may be granted if a first ranking hypothecary security bearing 5 per cent interest is established.
6. The purchaser shall pay a deposit of one-fifth of the purchase price as soon as the contract of purchase and sale with the natives or, in the case of ownerless land, the occupation deed has been submitted to the Government, and the latter has notified him that there are no objections to the selected land being taken into use. This notification has also to fix the purchase price, and to make a decision as to a deposit and any special conditions (see also No. 10). The notification shall be served against receipt. The amount paid will be refunded if the land is not transferred subsequently because of circumstances for which the purchaser is not responsible. The balance of the purchase price is to be paid before the date of the real conveyance, unless, by way of exception, respite has been granted in return for the payment of a security. Evidence of payment must be shown at the hearing.
7. The purchaser is to begin clearing and cultivating the land or putting it

to some other agricultural use within one year of the date of the notification mentioned in No. 6, failing which the ownership granted him will revert free of charge to the Treasury.

The purchaser is further obliged to clear and cultivate, or to take and maintain in another form of permanent use, in accordance with the principles of tropical agriculture or animal husbandry, one-fifth of the acquired land within five years, reckoned from that date, and three-quarters within fifteen years.

In assessing the area utilised, land on which structures of lasting value have been erected shall be counted tenfold.

8. If the land is not transferred because of circumstances for which the Treasury is responsible, the purchaser will be compensated for expenditure after the notification mentioned in No. 6, insofar as it has increased the value of the land.

9. If, at the request of the vendor, the purchaser does not prove at the latest during the first half of the sixth or sixteenth year respectively that he has fulfilled the obligations stipulated above, or that he has been prevented from fulfilling them by circumstances for which he is not responsible, the entire area which has not been cleared will revert free of charge to the Treasury, without claim to a refund of the purchase price and the cost of acquiring the land.

10. For land which is not acquired for agricultural purposes, special conditions can be imposed instead of the compulsory utilisation of the land.

11. The purchaser is under obligation to cede to the Treasury free of charge land required for roads, railways, telegraphs, telephones, wireless stations, sea-marks, beacons, landing-places and other public installations and institutions.

    If the clearing or cultivating of land resumed under this provision has already begun, the cost of clearing or cultivating is to be refunded, insofar as satisfactory evidence can be produced and insofar as the value of the land has been increased thereby.

12. The purchaser is obliged to suffer the drainage of water from public roads onto and across his land without claim to compensation. The purchaser is obliged to keep the boundaries of his land permanently marked and open, as far as they were blazed.

13. Public roads touching or traversing the land and existing landing places are to be acknowledged as such. Public roads and roads giving access to them, no matter whether already in existence or to be built in the future, must be maintained. The natives cannot be prohibited from using the beach as a road, landing-place or fishing ground.

14. When the entry is made in the Ground Book, the purchaser must

consent to a caution in accordance with B.G.B., S.883 being entered to safeguard the rights which are reserved to the Treasury in accordance with Nos. 1, 5, 6, 7, 9, 11, 12, 13 and 15.

15. If the purchaser re-transfers the land, he remains liable for the fulfilment of the obligations agreed to in the contract of purchase and sale by the third party, until the latter has entered into a legally binding obligation in relation to the Treasury and undertaken to transfer ownership only on condition that the acquirer enters into the same obligations to the Treasury.

V

Transfer of land under eased conditions (Form C)

1. Blocks of government land of up to 150 hectares can be transferred for a purchase price of 1 mark per hectare, or portions thereof, and without charging for the acquisition, survey and real conveyance, to such applicants as have been resident in the Protectorate for one year, or for two years in another tropical country, who wish to settle independently, who have not yet acquired land in the Protectorate, who are at least 21 years old and physically fit for the work of a planter in the Protectorate.
2. The applicant shall first be allowed to use the land free of charge. The real conveyance shall take place when the settler has lived on the land continuously for three years and has cleared, cultivated or otherwise taken and permanently maintained in use, in accordance with the principles of tropical agriculture, at least one-fifth of the land, provided the conditions for the entry in the Ground Book are met.
3. The applicant must bind himself to erect on the land a homestead suitable for Europeans from which the plantation can be managed, to live permanently in it until the real conveyance of the land has been effected and to continue to live there afterwards, or to arrange that another European, as a rule a subject of the Reich, takes up permanent residence there. If he fails to fulfil this obligation, the land will revert to the Treasury without compensation.
4. This type of land transfer shall only take place in areas which have been expressly chosen for it. The extension of such farms by the purchase of additional government land shall not be allowed on principle. Only in special cases are large plantations to be permitted in such areas.
5. The transfer of ownership of the land, or the right to use it in another way is permitted only with the approval of the Government. Permission must be given for this restriction to be entered into the Ground Book.
6. The general conditions apply insofar as nothing to the contrary has been directed.

VI

Leasing of land. In general

The preceding provisions under I to IV are correspondingly applicable to the lease of land, unless directions to the contrary are given.

VII

Leasing of government land in built up areas (Form D) and for establishing permanent trading stations etc. (Form E)

Land of the type defined above in II, Nos. 3, 4, 5 and 6 shall be leased under the following general conditions:

1. The lease shall be for a term of thirty years.
2. The rent for land in built up areas shall be determined for the first five years for each individual case, depending on the development of the settlement. In Rabaul it is, at present, 2 marks per are, or portions thereof.
3. Otherwise the rent for the first five years, commencing from the date of the beginning of the lease, shall be at least 20 marks per year per hectare, or portions thereof in the case of land with a sea-frontage, and 10 marks per year and hectare, or portions thereof for other land.
4. If land is leased for trading stations in areas which, in the opinion of the local administrative authority, are to be regarded as having been opened up, the rent will amount to at least 100 marks per year per hectare, or portions thereof; in the case of land with a sea-frontage the rent will rise to at least 150 marks per year per hectare, or portions thereof.
5. If a small plantation is to be combined with a trading station, for which adjacent bush will be cultivated, this rent can be reduced by up to half of the given rates.
6. The rent is to be paid each year in advance and falls due on 1st April, unless otherwise stipulated.
7. The rent for the next five years and then again for the last twenty years shall be determined by a Commission, to which the lessor and lessee shall each appoint two members. The members elect a chairman. If they cannot agree, the chairman will be appointed by the Imperial District Judge. The Commission shall meet, at the instance of one of the parties, three months before the respective five year period has expired. The rent shall be fixed by the Commission with due regard to the location of the land and its suitability for the erection of private, commercial or trade premises and not according to the value of the buildings and installations actually erected on the land.
8. If the lessee regards the rent determined by the Commission as too high,

he can terminate the lease by giving one year's notice within four weeks of the Commission's decision being announced. Conversely the lessor has the same right. When the rent is fixed a second time (after ten years), it will apply to the last twenty years of the lease.

9. The lessee shall bear the cost of acquiring the land for the Treasury by occupying it or purchasing it from natives. The Treasury shall bear the costs of the survey and of the entry in the Ground Book.
10. The legal or equitable subletting of the lease to third parties and the succession of heirs upon the death of the lessee is governed by the *Civil Code.*
11. Depending on the circumstances of the case, and with the approval of the lessee, it can be stipulated that the Treasury has the option of terminating the lease upon the death of the lessee.
12. Within six months the lessee is to clear and keep clean the leased land and, where necessary, plant it with cultivated grass. He must also drain or fill in any waterholes, pools and swampy areas on it and erect and maintain during the term of the lease at his expense all installations the public health authorities may deem to be necessary to remove health hazards from the land (for instance, by connecting the land to a water supply and sewerage system).
    Easier conditions can be stipulated for land outside built up areas.
13. Public roads touching or traversing the land and existing landing places must be acknowledged as such. Public roads, as well as roads giving access to them, no matter whether already in existence or to be built in the future, must be maintained.
14. The type of use the lessee intends to make of the land shall be defined in the lease. The lessee must take the leased land into use within a year of the execution of the lease and must erect on it whatever buildings are necessary for this purpose.
15. From the beginning of the second year of the lease only high quality materials, such as stone, earth, cement, timber, corrugated iron, slate etc. may be used for buildings on the type of land defined in II, No. 3. Materials liable to deteriorate quickly, such as leaves, mats, bamboo etc. may not be used. Temporary structures shall be excepted. Existing building regulations are not affected by this provision.
16. The lessor is not liable for the accuracy of the area assumed in the lease.
17. As soon as the need arises, building plans for built up areas shall be prepared. In these a section shall be set aside as a residential area for natives. In urban areas only land in this part may be transferred to them.
18, Buildings erected outside the native quarter cannot be used as dwellings for natives, unless these are employed in the household of a European

or a person of equal status, or have been appointed as guards outside business hours on land on which no such person resides.

These provisions also apply to persons whose status is equal to that of natives. Without special permission of the authorities, leases within the native quarter cannot be used as a residence by a non-native who does not have native status.

19. On termination of the lease the Treasury will not pay compensation for expenditure incurred in relation to the land. The lessee may, and, if requested, must remove all structures erected on the land unless the Treasury exercises its option to take over the buildings at the value they still represent at the time of the takeover. If no agreement is reached on this value, it will be determined by a Commission to be set up in accordance with No. 5.

20. If the lessee falls into arrears in fulfilling any of his contractual obligations, the lessor is entitled to terminate the lease forthwith.

21. The lease contract is to be executed in writing or before a public authority. The lessee shall bear the costs of the documentary authentication.

VIII

Lease of land which remains the property of the natives (Form F)

1. Only smaller blocks of native land which are to be used temporarily, for instance for practising a trade, or for commerce, or for the purposes of an expedition and the like, shall be leased by the Treasury for sub-letting to private persons.
2. The lease contract between the Treasury and the subtenant must be executed in writing or before a public authority.
3. The Treasury is not liable for the accuracy of the area assumed in the contract. The land can be used only for the purpose stipulated in the lease. If the land is used contrary to the stipulation, the Government is entitled to terminate the lease forthwith.
4. The term of the lease shall be no more than five years. The Treasury is free to terminate the lease before expiry of the term by giving one year's notice. The subtenant is to pay a fee to the Treasury, as well as to the owner of the land, which is due each year in advance on 1st April. For land with a sea-frontage the rent shall amount to at least 30 marks per hectare, or portions thereof, and for other land at least 25 marks. Two-thirds of the rent is to be paid to the Treasury, one-third to the natives.

   If land is leased for the establishment of a trading station in areas which, in the opinion of the local administrative authority, are to be regarded as opened up, the rent will amount to at least 150 marks per year and per hectare, or portions thereof. For land with a sea-frontage the rent will increase to at least 200 marks per year and per hectare, or portions thereof. Four-fifths of the rent is to be paid to the Treasury, one-fifth to the natives.

5. It is not possible to renew such a lease after the first term has expired. But a new lease can be executed in accordance with VII, after the Treasury has acquired ownership of the land.
6. On termination of the lease the Treasury will not pay compensation for expenditure incurred in relation to the land. The subtenant may remove any structures erected on the land; at the request of the owner he must do so free of charge.
7. The lease and sublease are otherwise governed by the *Civil Code*.

IX

Lease of government land to Europeans and persons of equal status for plantations (Form G)

In so far as nothing is directed to the contrary, land shall be leased for plantations under the following general conditions:

1. The area of land to be leased shall be, in principle, not less than 50 hectares.
   Small islands and leased blocks adjoining land already owned by the lessee are excepted.
2. The term of the lease shall be thirty years.
3. The lessee shall bear the cost of acquiring the land for the Treasury.
4. The Treasury shall bear the cost of the survey, demarcation and entry in the Ground Book.
5. The rent is to be paid each year in advance and is due on 1st April, unless otherwise stipulated. It shall amount, in principle, to 0.20 marks per hectare, or portions thereof. The right is reserved to stipulate in individual cases a higher amount, on account of location, type of soil and intended use, or to waive the rent completely for the first ten years. No guarantee whatsoever is given that the selected land is suitable for the purpose for which the acquirer intends to use it.
6. The lessee is obliged to commence clearing and cultivating the land or putting it to some other agricultural use within one year of executing the lease.
7. The lessee is further obliged to clear and cultivate, or to take and maintain in another form of permanent use, in accordance with the principles of tropical agriculture, one-fifth of the land within five years of executing the lease, and three-quarters within fifteen years.
   To prevent the impoverishment of the soil etc., depending on the kind

of cultivation, special obligations to manage the land prudently can be imposed on the lessee in the lease.

8. The legal or equitable subletting of the lease to third parties and the succession of heirs upon the death of the lessee is governed by the *Civil Code.*
9. The lessor is not liable for the land having the size assumed in the lease, even if the land has been surveyed.
10. If a subsequent survey shows that the land falls short of, or exceeds the size assumed in the lease, the rent is to be correspondingly reduced or increased and the difference paid. Rent which has been overpaid in the past shall be credited against future rents. If agreement is reached that the deficiency is to be made up by assigning other land for lease to the lessee, the original amount of rent is to be paid in the future, irrespective of a deduction of the amounts which have been overpaid up till the subsequent survey. The lessee has no claim to be assigned land for lease elsewhere.
11. The lessor does not guarantee that the land is not subject to rights of third parties.
12. The lessor is entitled to terminate the lease at any time in respect of those sections of the land which are required for the building of roads, railways, telegraph and telephone installations, sea-marks, beacons, wireless stations, landing-places and other public installations.
    If the clearing and cultivating of land resumed under this provision has already begun, the cost of clearing and cultivating will be refunded, but taking into account the profits the lessee has already derived from its use. No further compensation shall be granted.
13. The lessee is obliged to suffer the drainage of water from public roads onto and across the land without claim to compensation. Public roads touching or traversing the land and existing landing-places are to be acknowledged as such. Public roads and roads giving access to them, no matter whether already in existence or to be built in the future, must be maintained.
14. On termination of the lease the lessor will not pay the lessee any compensation for expenditure incurred in relation to the land. The lessee may and, if requested, must remove any structures erected on the land.
15. If the lessee falls into arrears in fulfilling his contractual obligations, the lessor is entitled to terminate the lease forthwith.
16. The prospect of a renewal of his lease for a further thirty years for a rent which should not exceed 40 marks per hectare will be offered the lessee, if he punctually fulfils all his contractual obligations during the period of the lease.

17. The lease contract is to be executed in writing or before a public authority. The lessor shall bear the costs of the documentary authentication.

X

Lease of government land for plantations to persons who do not have the status of Europeans (Form G)

1 Certain areas of the Protectorate shall be set aside for the establishment of plantations by persons who do not have the status of Europeans. For this purpose areas which are uninhabited, or only sparsely inhabited and whose topography renders them unsuitable for large plantations shall be considered.

2. The size of the leased land shall, as a rule, be at least 10 hectares. It shall, in principle, not exceed 50 hectares.

3. The term of the lease shall be thirty years.

4. The lessee is to bear the cost of acquiring the land for the Treasury.

5. The Treasury shall bear the cost of any survey, demarcation and entry into the Ground Book.

6. The rent is to be paid each year in advance, and falls due on 1st April, unless otherwise stipulated. It shall be 1 mark per hectare for each of the first three years, 2 marks during the subsequent three years and increase in this way by 1 mark per hectare every three years.

7. The lessee is obliged to commence clearing and cultivating the land, or putting it to some other agricultural use, within one year of executing the lease.

8. The lessee is further obliged to clear and cultivate the land within five years, or to take and maintain it in another form of permanent use, in accordance with the principles of tropical agriculture.
To prevent the impoverishment of the soil etc., depending on the kind of cultivation, special obligations to manage the land prudently can be imposed on the lessee in the lease.

9. The legal or equitable subletting of the lease to third parties and the succession of heirs upon the death of the lessee is governed by the *Civil Code.*

10. The lessor is not liable for the accuracy of the area assumed in the lease or any survey.
If a subsequent survey shows that the land falls short of, or exceeds the area assumed in the lease, the rent will be reduced or increased correspondingly and the difference paid. Rent which has been overpaid in the past shall be credited against future rents. If agreement is reached that the deficiency is to be made up by assigning other land for lease to

the lessee, the original amount of rent is to be paid in the future, irrespective of a deduction of the amounts which have been overpaid up till the subsequent survey. The lessee has no claim to be assigned land for lease elsewhere.

The lessor does not guarantee that the land is not subject to rights of third parties.

11. The lessor is entitled to terminate the lease at any time in respect of those sections of the land which are required for the building of roads, railways, telegraph and telephone installations, sea-marks, beacons, wireless stations, landing-places and other public installations.

    If the clearing and cultivating of land resumed under this provision has already begun, the cost of clearing and cultivating is to be refunded, but taking into account the profits the lessee has already derived from its use. No further compensation shall be granted.
12. The lessee is obliged to suffer the drainage of water from public roads onto and across the land without claim to compensation. Public roads touching or traversing the land and existing landing-places must be acknowledged as such. Public roads and roads giving access to them, no matter whether already in existence or to be built in the future, must be maintained.
13. On termination of the lease the lessor will not pay the lessee any compensation for expenditure incurred in relation to the land. The lessee may and, if requested, must remove any structures erected on the land.
14. The prospect of a renewal of his lease for a further thirty years for a rent which should not exceed 40 marks per hectare will be offered to the lessee, if he punctually fulfils all his contractual obligations during the period of the lease.
15. If the lessee falls into arrears in fulfilling his contractual obligations, the lessor is entitled to terminate the lease forthwith.
16. The lease is to be executed in writing or before a public authority. The lessor shall bear the costs of the documentary authentication.

Final Remarks

The principles set out above do not constitute binding regulations. They give no applicant a claim to acquire land by way of purchase or lease. The Government reserves the right to amend these conditions at any time or to impose special conditions in individual cases.

PRINCIPLES FOR THE TRANSFER OF LAND IN THE PROTECTORATE OF GERMAN NEW GUINEA, INCLUDING THE ISLAND TERRITORY, OF 1st JANUARY 1914*

I

The acquisition of land or real rights to land by occupying ownerless land or by contracts with the natives has been by statute reserved to the Treasury. No contracts between non-natives or non-indigenous natives and the natives of the Protectorate regarding the acquisition of land or real rights to land shall be ratified.

Nor shall contracts with natives be ratified which concern the use of native land, unless exceptions arise out of VI below.

In administratively organised areas the acquisition of land for the Treasury by occupying ownerless land or by contract with natives shall be carried out by or with the assistance of an official of the Protectorate. Outside administratively organised areas other persons can be authorised to acquire land for the Treasury.

If the land has not been selected within a year of the date of issue of the authority, the authority will become ineffective. The expenses of the authorised person shall not be refunded.

The transfer of government land acquired in this way is governed by the following principles.

II

Restrictions regarding the land to be transferred [1]

The following types of land are excluded from transfer into private ownership:

1. Land which is used by the public: public roads, public landing-places, public wells, market places, springs, navigable rivers etc.
2. Land which is inhabited by natives or has been taken into agricultural use by them, land which natives require to construct and house their sea-craft and fishing-tackle – taking into account that it must remain

---

* These Principles were not published in any of the collections of German colonial law. A photocopy of the original on which this translation is based has been deposited in the library of the Supreme Court of Papua New Guinea

1 See Fn. 1, p.58.

possible for the natives to use boats and cutters as sea-craft – uninhabited small islands which the natives use as resting places while fishing. Land which has been set aside as a native reserve. When native reserves are set aside, wherever practicable, at least one hectare of land suitable for the planting of garden crops and coconut palms is to be allowed per head of the native population.

3. Land in the vicinity of government posts and urban settlements.
4. Coastal land in the vicinity of important harbours and landing-places as well as at the mouth of navigable rivers.
5. Small blocks of land which, on account of their location and size, are suitable only for the erection of trading stations without plantations directly attached.
6. Land which in its original state, that is without being cleared and cultivated, already yields a sufficient quantity of produce to warrant permanent management. This will depend on whether the useful plants already there can produce, in the long term, sufficient returns to cover, from the outset, a substantial part of the costs of proper management and of increasing the returns in the future.
   A lease or the right to use land of the type described above, shall be granted under specially stipulated conditions.
7. Land which is more suited for forestry than for agricultural use. The Protectorate's stocks of useful and fine timbers not situated on private property shall be exploited by the granting of temporary timber cutting rights which shall be restricted in accordance with the principles of forestry.

III

Principles regarding the person of the applicant

1. As a rule government land shall not be transferred into the ownership of natives or persons of equal status.
2. Persons other than those defined in No. 1. are excluded from buying or leasing government land, if they are not able to read and write a European language.
3. With the exception of the cases defined in VIII, Nos. 1 and 2, government land shall not be sold or leased to subjects of states where the acquisition of land by citizens of the Reich is restricted.

Companies, legal persons.

4. Companies or legal persons are only allowed to buy or lease government land if they have been incorporated in accordance with German law in Germany or a German Protectorate.

The transfer of land at reduced prices

5. At reduced prices and without charging for the acquisition, survey and real conveyance, blocks of about 100 hectares of government land (if possible in the form of rectangles) shall be transferred to such applicants as have been resident in the Protectorate for one year, or for two years in another tropical country, who wish to settle independently, who have not yet acquired land in the Protectorate, who are at least 21 years old and physically fit for the work of a planter in the Protectorate.
The applicant shall first be allowed to use the land free of charge. The real conveyance shall take place when the settler has lived on the land continuously for three years and has cleared and cultivated, or otherwise taken and permanently maintained in use, in accordance with the principles of tropical agriculture, at least one-fifth of the land.

Size of blocks

6. Each block of land shall comprise at least 100 hectares and, as far as possible, be rectangular, unless the coastline, river banks and roads suggest that another shape is more suitable, or unless this is necessitated by natural boundaries.
Even in the case of larger land acquisitions continuous blocks are to be selected wherever possible. If, for special reasons, land is acquired in several places, each block shall comprise at least 500 hectares.
The land shall not extend for more than 2 metres per hectare along the coast or along the bank of a navigable river.

Working capital

7. The purchaser must show that he possesses a working capital of 20,000 marks in cash or unencumbered profitable investments for every 100 hectares he wishes to acquire.

Mission societies

8. Subject to the existing special regulations, mission societies do not have to show the availability of a working capital for land which is to serve directly for the purpose of worship or instruction.
Such land can be transferred only with the approval of the Government.
The purchase price shall also be determined by special regulation.

Subsequent purchase of leased land

9. Lessees of government land who are neither natives nor of equal status can be permitted to buy, after the expiry of the lease, those portions of the land which they have cleared and planted during the term of the lease without regard to Nos. 6 and 7.

IV[1]

General conditions for the sale of land

Government land shall be sold under the following general conditions:

Surveys

1. No guarantee is given that the land is of the size assumed at the sale, even if it has been surveyed. If the land was not surveyed at the time of the sale, the purchaser is under obligation to have the land surveyed later by a certified surveyor at his own expense, and in accordance with the special regulations existing for such cases, if he is requested to do so: a) if for some reason such a surveyor comes to the area in question and if the re-survey can be carried out without undue difficulty; b) if another person acquires ownership of land adjoining the first block.

   The owner of the land must accept as final any later determination of the boundaries by a certified surveyor and has no claim against the Treasury or adjoining owner if the size of his block is altered. He has no claim for damages against the Treasury for any errors in the original survey and is liable to the Treasury if claims are made against it by third parties because of such errors. On request the purchaser must establish a cautionary hypothec to secure the fulfilment of the above obligations.

Rights of third parties

2. Duly acquired rights by third parties to the land sold are protected. The Treasury does not guarantee that the land sold is not subject to rights of third parties.

Purchase price

3. The purchase price shall be determined according to the location of the land, the type of soil and its intended use and at present amounts, as a rule, to 5 marks per hectare.

   If unsurveyed land is sold and a certain area is stated, the purchase price will be correspondingly reduced or increased, if a later survey shows that the land falls short of, or exceeds the area assumed at the sale. If the area is deficient, the purchaser can be assigned other land to make

---

* The German original says 'VI' instead of 'IV', but this is clearly a printing error.

up the deficiency, instead of being refunded part of the purchase price. The purchaser has no claim to be assigned such land elsewhere.

4.[1] The purchaser shall bear the cost of acquiring the land by contract with the natives or of occupying ownerless land and shall supply the necessary labour and services for the boundaries to be preliminarily fixed. He also bears the cost of the survey and demarcation, as well as the costs of the real conveyance and entry in the Ground Book. These incidental expenses must be paid at once, with the exception of the cost of the survey for which respite of payment may be granted if a first ranking hypothecary security is established.

Duty to utilise the land

5. The purchaser is to begin clearing and cultivating the land, or putting it to some other agricultural use within one year of the contract being executed, failing which he is bound to re-transfer to the Treasury the ownership granted him.

The purchaser is further obliged to clear and cultivate, or to take and maintain in another form of permanent use, in accordance with the principles of tropical agriculture or animal husbandry, three-quarters of the acquired land within fifteen years of the date on which the contract was executed.

In assessing the area utilised, land on which structures of lasting value have been erected shall be counted tenfold.

If at the request of the vendor, the purchaser does not prove at the latest during the first half of the sixteenth year that he has fulfilled the obligations stipulated above, or that he has been prevented from fulfilling them by circumstances for which he is not responsible, he is to re-transfer free of charge to the Treasury the entire area which has not been cleared, without claim to a refund of the purchase price and the cost of acquiring the land.

For land which is not acquired for agricultural purposes, special conditions can be imposed instead of the compulsory utilisation of the land.

---

* No. 4 was by mistake omitted from the printed form. It was added by hand in the original on which this translation is based. The German original speaks of vendor (Verkäufer) instead of purchaser (Käufer), but the context as well as a comparison with the 1912 Principles (IV, 5) clearly show that this is an error.

Expropriation proviso

6. The purchaser is under obligation to cede to the Treasury free of charge land required for roads, railways, telegraph installations, telephone installations, wireless stations, sea-marks, beacons, landing-places and other public installations or institutions.
   If the clearing or cultivating of land resumed under this provision has already begun, the cost of clearing or cultivating is to be refunded, in so far as satisfactory evidence can be produced and in so far as the value of the land has been increased thereby.
7. The purchaser is obliged to suffer the drainage of water from public roads onto and across his land without claim to compensation.
   The purchaser is obliged to keep the boundaries of his land permanently marked and open, as far as they were blazed.
8. Public roads and landing-places existing on the land must be acknowledged as such. Public roads and roads giving access to them, no matter whether already in existence or to be built in the future, must be maintained to the width prescribed by the administrative authorities. In the case of main roads the width is usually 6 metres. This obligation does not apply to roads for whose maintenance the Treasury will take or has expressly taken responsibility.
9. When entry is made in the Ground Book, the purchaser must consent to a caution in accordance with B.G.B., S.883 being entered to safeguard the rights which are reserved to the Treasury in accordance with Nos. 1, 5, 6, 7, 8 and 10.[1]
10. If the purchaser re-transfers the land, he remains liable for the fulfilment of the obligations agreed to in the contract of purchase and sale by the third party, until the latter has entered into a legally binding obligation in relation to the Treasury and undertakes to transfer ownership only on condition that the acquirer enters into the same obligations to the Treasury.

V

General conditions for the transfer of land at reduced prices

When land is transferred according to III, Nos. 5 and 8, IV also applies, unless special provisions are made elsewhere in these Principles (purchase price, waiving of survey costs, etc.).

---

* The German original says '11' instead of '10', but this is clearly a printing error.

In these cases the following special conditions apply: the transfer of ownership or rights to use the land in any other form shall be subject to approval by the Government; the entry of this restriction in the Ground Book must be consented to.

VI

Lease of native land

As a rule the Treasury does not lease native land for the purpose of sub-letting it to private persons. It is admissible if the land is to be used for establishing a mission station, or a commercial enterprise, or for the purpose of an expedition or like objectives.

The acquisition of native land by way of lease is governed by the provisions laid down for acquiring ownership of native land.

The lease between the Treasury and the subtenant must be executed in writing, or before a public authority.

The Treasury is not liable for the accuracy of the area assumed in the contract. The land can be used only for the purpose stipulated in the lease. If the land is used contrary to the stipulation, the Government is entitled to terminate the contract forthwith, without resorting to court action.

Apart from the rent to be paid to the owner of the land, the subtenant must pay a fee which is to be determined for each individual case. It must be paid each year in advance and falls due on 1st April, unless otherwise stipulated. On termination of the lease the Treasury will not pay compensation for expenditure incurred in relation to the land. The subtenant may remove any structures erected on the land; he must do so at the request of the owner.

The lease and sublease are otherwise governed by the *Civil Code.*

VII

Lease of urban land

Land of the type defined in II, Nos. 3, 4 and 5 shall be leased under the following general conditions:

1. The lease shall be for a term of thirty years.
2. The rent for the first five years, commencing from the date of the beginning of the lease, shall be 20 marks per year per hectare in the case of land with a sea-frontage, but at least 10 marks per year, and in the case of other land 10 marks per year per hectare, but at least 5 marks per year.

   The rent is to be paid each year in advance and falls due on 1st April, unless otherwise stipulated. The rent for the next five years and then again for the last twenty years shall be determined by a Commission to which the lessee and lessor shall each appoint two members. The members elect a chairman. If they cannot agree, the chairman will be appointed by the Imperial District Judge. The Commission shall meet, at the instance of one of the parties, three months before the respective five year period has expired.

The rent shall be fixed by the Commission with due regard to the location of the land and its suitability for the erection of private, commercial or trade premises on it and not according to the value of the buildings actually erected on the land.

If the lessee regards the rent determined by the Commission as too high, he can terminate the lease by giving one year's notice within four weeks of the Commission's decision being announced. Conversely the lessor has the same right. When the rent is fixed a second time (after ten years), it will apply to the last twenty years of the lease.

Incidental expenses

3. The lessee shall bear the cost of acquiring the land for the Treasury by occupying it or purchasing it from natives. The Treasury shall bear the cost of the survey and of the entry in the Ground Book.

Sublease

4. The legal or equitable subletting of the lease to third parties and the succession of heirs upon the death of the lessee is governed by the *Civil Code.*

Sanitary measures

5. The lessee is to bind himself to clear and keep clean the leased land within six months, and where necessary, to plant it with cultivated grass. He must also drain or fill in any waterholes, pools and swampy areas on it and erect and maintain during the term of the lease at his expense all installations the public health authorities may deem to be necessary to remove health hazards from the land (for instance, by connecting the land to a water supply and sewerage system).

Public roads and landing-places existing on the land must be acknowledged as such. Public roads and roads giving access to them, no matter whether already in existence or to be built in the future, must be maintained to the width prescribed by the administrative authorities. In the case of main roads the width is usually 6 metres. This obligation does not apply to roads for whose maintenance the Treasury has expressly taken or will take responsibility.

6. The type of use the lessee intends to make of the land shall be defined in the lease. The lessee must take the leased land into use within two years of the lease being executed and must erect on it whatever buildings are necessary for this purpose.
7. From the beginning of the second year of the lease only high quality materials, such as stone, earth, cement, corrugated iron, slate etc. may be used for buildings on the type of land defined in II, No. 3. Materials liable to deteriorate quickly, such as leaves, mats, bamboo etc., may not be used. Temporary structures shall be excepted. Existing building regulations are not affected by this provision.
8. The lessor is not liable for the accuracy of the area assumed in the lease.
9. As soon as the need arises, building plans for built up areas shall be prepared. In these a section shall be set aside as a residential area for natives. In urban areas only land in this part may be transferred to them.
   Buildings erected outside the native quarter cannot be used as dwellings for natives, unless these are employed in the household of a non-native or a person of non-native status, or have been appointed as guards outside business hours on land on which no such person resides. The second sentence of the preceding paragraph, also applies to persons of native status.
   Without special permission of the authorities leases within the native quarter cannot be used as a residence by a non-native who does not have native status.
10. On termination of the lease the Treasury will not pay compensation for expenditure incurred in relation to the land. The lessee may remove all structures from the land, unless the Treasury exercises its option to take over the buildings at the value they still represent at the time of the take-over. If no agreement is reached on this value, it will be determined by a Commission to be set up in accordance with VII, No.2.
11. The lease contract is to be executed in writing or before the Imperial District Judge or his representative. The lessee shall bear the costs of the documentary authentication.

VIII

Lease of land to persons of native status

1. Certain areas of the Protectorate shall be set aside for the establishment of plantations by persons who have the same status as natives.
   For this purpose areas which are uninhabited, or only sparsely inhabited and whose topography renders them unsuitable for large plantations are to be selected.

2. Land for plantation purposes shall be leased to persons of native status only in those areas of the Protectorate defined in No. 1.
3. The size of the lease shall, as a rule, be at least 10 hectares.
4. The term of the lease shall be thirty years.
5. The lessee is to bear the cost of acquiring the land for the Treasury.
6. The Treasury shall bear the cost of any survey, demarcation and entry in the Ground Book.
7. The rent is to be paid each year in advance and falls due on 1st April, unless otherwise stipulated. It shall be 1 mark per hectare for each of the first three years, to 2 marks during the subsequent three years and increase in this way by 1 mark per hectare every three years.
8. The lessee is obliged to commence clearing and cultivating the land, or putting it to some other agricultural use, within six months of executing the lease.
9. The lessee is further obliged to clear and cultivate the land within five years, or to take and maintain it in another form of permanent use, in accordance with the principles of tropical agriculture.
10. The legal or equitable subletting of the lease to third parties and the succession of heirs upon the death of the lessee are governed by the *Civil Code.*
11. The lessor is not liable for the accuracy of the area assumed in the lease or any survey.
    The lessor does not guarantee that the land is not subject to rights of third parties.
12. The lessor is entitled to terminate the lease at any time in respect of those sections of the land which are required for the building of roads, railways, telegraph and telephone installations, sea-marks, beacons, wireless stations, landing-places and other public installations. If the clearing and cultivating of land resumed under this provision has already begun, the cost of clearing and cultivating the land is to be refunded, but taking into account the profits the lessee has already derived from its use. No further compensation than that mentioned in the preceding paragraph shall be granted.
13. The lessee is obliged to suffer the drainage of water from public roads onto and across the land without claim to compensation. Public roads and landing-places existing on the land must be acknowledged as such. Public roads and roads giving access to them, no matter whether already in existence or to be built in the future, must be maintained to the width prescribed by the administrative authorities. In the case of main roads the width is usually 6 metres. This obligation does not apply to roads for whose maintenance the Treasury will take or has expressly taken responsibility.

14. On termination of the lease the lessor will not pay the lessee any compensation for expenditure incurred in relation to the land. The lessee may and, if requested, must remove any structures erected on the land.
15. The prospect of a renewal of his lease for a further thirty years for a rent which should not exceed 20 marks per hectare will be offered to the lessee, if he punctually fulfils all his contractual obligations during the period of the lease.
16. The right of the lessor to terminate the lease, if the lessee does not fulfil his contractual obligations, is governed by the *Civil Code.*

IX

Lease of plantation land to non-natives or persons of non-native status

In so far as the preceding provisions do not contain directions to the contrary, land shall be leased for plantations under the following general conditions:

1. The area of the land to be leased shall be, as a rule, not less than 50 hectares. The block should, if possible, be rectangular.
   Small islands and leased blocks adjoining land already owned by the lessee are excepted.
2. The term of the lease shall be thirty years.
3. The lessee shall bear the cost of acquiring the land for the Treasury.
4. The Treasury shall bear the cost of the survey, demarcation and entry in the Ground Book.
5. The rent is to be paid each year in advance and is due on 1st April, unless otherwise stipulated. It shall be determined according to the location of the land, the type of soil and its intended use.
6. The lessee is obliged to commence clearing and cultivating the land or putting it to some other agricultural use within two years of executing the lease.
7. The lessee is further obliged to clear and cultivate, or to take and maintain in another form of permanent use, in accordance with the principles of tropical agriculture, not less than three-quarters of the land within fifteen years of executing the lease.
8. The legal or equitable subletting of the lease to third parties and the succession of heirs upon the death of the lessee is governed by the *Civic Code.*
9. The lessor is not liable for the land having the size assumed in the lease, if government land is leased which has not been surveyed by a certified surveyor and linked to an established trigonometrical grid.

In this case the lessee cannot claim compensation from the Treasury for errors in the survey.

10. If a subsequent survey shows that the land falls short of, or exceeds the size assumed in the lease, the rent is to be correspondingly reduced or the difference paid. Rent which has been overpaid in the past shall be credited against future rents, unless an agreement is reached that the deficiency is to be made up by assigning other land for lease. The lessee has however no claim to be assigned such land for lease elsewhere.
11. The lessor does not guarantee that the land is not subject to rights of third parties.
12. The lessor is entitled to terminate the lease at any time in respect of those sections of the land which are required for the building of roads, railways, telegraph and telephone installations, sea-marks, beacons, wireless stations, landing-places and other public installations.
    If the clearing and cultivating of land resumed under this provision has already begun, the cost of clearing and cultivating the land is to be refunded, but taking into account the profits the lessee has already derived from its use. No further compensation than that mentioned in the preceding paragraph shall be granted.
13. The lessee is obliged to suffer the drainage of water from public roads onto and across his land without claim to compensation. Public roads and landing-places existing on the land must be acknowledged as such. Public roads and roads giving access to them, no matter whether already in existence or to be built in the future, must be maintained to the width prescribed by the administrative authorities. In the case of main roads the width is usually 6 metres. This obligation does not apply to roads for whose maintenance the Treasury will take or has expressly taken responsibility.
14. On termination of the lease the lessor will not pay the lessee any compensation for expenditure incurred in relation to the land. The lessee may and, if requested, must remove any structures erected on the land.
15. The right of the lessor to terminate the lease if the lessee does not fulfil his contractual obligations is governed by the *Civil Code.*
16. The prospect of a renewal of his lease for a further thirty years for a rent which should not exceed 20 marks per hectare will be offered to the lessee, if he punctually fulfils all his contractual obligations during the period of the lease.
17. The lease contract must be executed in writing or before the Imperial District Judge. The lessor shall bear the costs of the documentary authentication.

Final Remarks

The principles set out above do not constitute binding regulations. They give no applicant a claim to acquire land by way of purchase or lease. The Government reserves the right to amend these conditions at any time.

IMPERIAL ORDINANCE REGARDING THE EXPROPRIATION OF REAL PROPERTY IN THE AFRICAN AND PACIFIC PROTECTORATES, OF 14th FEBRUARY 1903*

We, Wilhelm, by the Grace of God German Emperor, King of Prussia etc., order by virtue of Section 3 of the *Protectorates' Act* (R.G. Bl., 1900, 813) in connection with Sections 20 and 21 of the *Statute Regarding Consular Jurisdiction,* of 7th April 1900 (R.G. Bl., 1900, 213), for the African and Pacific Protectorates as follows:

I. Admissibility and Conditions of Expropriation in General

Section 1

The ownership of land and all other rights to it, as well as mining rights and the right to occupy ownerless land (crown land), can, in the public interest, be resumed or restricted in return for compensation, in favour of enterprises which make it necessary to exercise the right of expropriation.

Section 2

The duty to pay compensation lies with the entrepreneur.

If the ownership of land is expropriated, the compensation will amount to the full value of the land. Instead of a cash payment other land can be granted as compensation. An increase in the value of the expropriated land resulting from the enterprise is not to be taken into account when calculating the compensation. If, as a result of the enterprise, there is an increase in the value of other land, which has remained the property of the owner, this increase shall be deducted from the compensation.

If the ownership is restricted, or if other rights are resumed or restricted, the compensation is to be calculated in cash in an equitable manner taking all circumstances into account. Subsection 2, Sentences 3 and 4, are correspondingly applicable.

---

* D.K.G., Vol. 7, 39-45.

Section 3

Apart from his duty to pay compensation, the entrepreneur must erect and maintain fences, installations for irrigation, drainage and the like, in so far as is necessary to protect adjacent land or the public from dangers and damages caused by the enterprise.

II. Expropriation Procedure

a) Institution of the procedure and granting of the right of expropriation

Section 4

Following the entrepreneur's application, which must state in general terms the purpose and extent of the enterprise, the Governor (Administrator) shall determine whether expropriation procedures are to be instituted.

The Governor can request a description, or even a plan of the enterprise to be supplied by a set date.

Section 5

If the institution of the procedure has been approved, the Governor is to make available for public inspection, through the competent District Office (Section 31), for an appropriate period of time, a description and, if in existence, also a plan of the enterprise. The period should not be less than one month. The commencement, duration and place of the publication must be announced in advance in accordance with local usage.

Section 6

During the period set according to Section 5, any parties concerned can lodge objections at the competent District Office, either in writing or by having an oral objection recorded.

Section 7

When the period has expired, the District Commissioner is to set a date for the hearing of the objections.

The date for the hearing is to be made public in accordance with local usage. The entrepreneur and all the parties known to be concerned are to be summoned to the hearing. The summons shall draw attention to the fact that the application for expropriation will be heard regardless of the non-appearance of a party concerned.

The District Commissioner can call witnesses and experts.

The District Commissioner must draw attention to the fact, that at the same hearing arrangements regarding the compensation will be made.

The proceedings are to be recorded.

Section 8

When the proceedings have been completed, the District Commissioner is to submit them to the Governor with an opinion as to whether or not the right of expropriation should be granted. The latter shall decide whether and to what extent the right of expropriation is to be granted.

The decision pronouncing the grant must state in detail:

a) the object of the expropriation, in particular the size and the boundaries of the land which may have to be resumed, the kind and the extent of possible restrictions, as well as the final date by which the right of expropriation must be exercised,

b) the installations which the entrepreneur is bound to erect and maintain (Section 3).

The decision is to be drawn up in writing and must give reasons. It must be served on the parties concerned and also made public in accordance with local usage.

b) Determination of the compensation

Section 9

When the decision granting the right of expropriation has been served on the entrepreneur, the District Commissioner must ask him to state, within a set period, what compensation he is prepared to pay.

Section 10

If the persons whose rights are affected by the expropriation are not yet known, the entrepreneur shall be responsible for obtaining the necessary evidence.

If he does not fulfil this obligation, the Governor can withdraw the right of expropriation following an application from the District Commissioner.

Section 11

The District Commissioner must set a date for a hearing regarding the compensation.

The date must be made public in accordance with local usage. This notice must contain the warning that a claim to compensation wil not be considered if the person of the holder of a right affected by the expropriation is not known before the hearing closes. The entrepreneur, the owner and all other known persons whose rights are affected by the expropriation must be summoned to the hearing. The summons should state that the compensation will be determined regardless of the non-appearance of a party concerned.

Section 12

If the attending parties agree on the compensation, the District Commissioner is to record their agreement.

Section 13

If possible, at least one expert is to be called *ex officio* to attend the hearing. In districts where communities have representative bodies, their opinion is also to be heard, if this is possible without causing undue delay.

Section 14

On the basis of the proceedings according to Sections 11 to 13, the District Commissioner shall determine the compensation in a decision stating his reasons.

The decision must state that the expropriation will only take place after the compensation has been paid, or security has been given. The decision must also state, that and in what manner a person entitled to receive the compensation must make a payment, or give security out of the compensation to other persons in respect of rights they hold to the land or right in question.

The decision is to be served on the parties concerned.

Section 15

If the determination of the compensation is not based on an agreement among the parties concerned, they have the right to appeal against the District Commissioner's decision within a month of its being served on them.

c) Execution of the expropriation

Section 16

Following an application by the entrepreneur, the District Commissioner shall order the expropriation, if the right of appeal (Section 15) has lapsed because of either the expiry of the one month period, or a binding judgment, or an act of renunciation, and if the compensation has been paid, or security for its payment given.

In case of great urgency the Governor can order, following an application by the entrepreneur, that the expropriation take place before the right of appeal has lapsed, as soon as the compensation has been paid in accordance with the decision determining it, or security for its payment has been given.

Section 17

The decision ordering the expropriation is to be served on the person entitled to compensation and on the entrepreneur. As soon as the decision has been served, the District Commissioner is to notify the Ground Book Office of the decision and of the date on which it was served on the person entitled to receive compensation.

d) Loss and surrender of the right of expropriation

Section 18

The right of expropriation lapses if the entrepreneur does not exercise it by the date set in Section 8, a), or if he withdraws from the enterprise before the compensation has been determined by the District Office. In this case the entrepreneur is liable in the course of law for all damages suffered by the person entitled to compensation as a result of the expropriation procedure.

If the entrepreneur withdraws after the compensation has been determined by the District Office, the person entitled to compensation will have the choice of demanding either compensation for the damages he has suffered as a result of the expropriation procedure, or of claiming compensation as determined, in which case he must cede the land or the rights which have been granted to the entrepreneur.

III. Effects of the Expropriation

Section 19

With the serving of the expropriation order on the person entitled to compensation, the entrepreneur acquires the ownership of the expropriated land or any other right granted to him in the order.

Section 20

As from the date defined in Section 19 the expropriated land or right shall be free of all rights which exist to the land or right in question, or which can be asserted against the owner or another rightholder, unless the continuation of such rights has been reserved in the expropriation order.

As regards ownership and other rights, the compensation payment shall take the place of the expropriated land or right.

IV. Simplification of the Procedure in Special Cases

a) Expropriation of materials contained in the soil

Section 21

If the expropriation is limited to the removal of materials for the building or the maintenance of public roads, the application for the institution of the expropriation procedure is to be made to the District Commissioner, or to be referred to him by the Governor. The District Commissioner is then to institute appropriate investigations regarding the amount of compensation which will probably have to be paid.

If he finds that the compensation will exceed the value of 1000 marks, he must transfer the matter to the Governor, who then acts in accordance with Section 4 ff., as if the entrepreneur had made his application to him.

If the District Commissioner is convinced that the compensation will not exceed the value of 1000 marks, he may grant the right of expropriation and at the same time determine the amount of compensation in a decision which must state his reasons.

Section 22

The parties concerned can lodge an objection with the Governor against this decision within a month of its being served on them.

This will not delay the execution of the decision.

To prepare their decisions, the District Commissioner and the Governor can hear witnesses and experts.

Section 19 is correspondingly applicable.

The right to remove materials will lapse if it is not exercised by the entrepreneur by a date to be set by the District Office.

b) Limitations on ownership for periods of less than one year

Section 23

If the entrepreneur applies for ownership of land to be restricted for only a certain period, not exceeding one year, the Governor can refer the application to the District Commissioner.

The District Commissioner shall then decide whether the right of expropriation be granted and on the amount of compensation to be paid. Reasons must be stated in the decision. Section 22, Subsections 1 to 3, and Section 19 are correspondingly applicable.

e) Expropriation of native rights

Section 24

If the expropriation is directed against a right held by natives, the District Commissioner, following an application by the entrepreneur, and after having carried out the investigations he considers appropriate, will make a decision, stating his reasons, on whether the right of expropriation be granted, the date by which it must be exercised and the kind and amount of compensation which is to be paid. Section 22, Subsections 1 to 3, and Section 19 are correspondingly applicable

V. Costs

Section 25

For the entire expropriation procedure heard before the administrative authorities the entrepreneur is to pay one fee according to schedule A of Section 57 of the *Prussian Statute Regarding the Costs of Court Actions* (P.G., 1899, 326).

The size of the fee shall depend on the amount of compensation which is finally determined.

For a decision on appeal the appellant has to pay a separate fee of at least 1 mark and no more than 20 marks, but in any case no more than half the fee according to Subsection 1, if his appeal is entirely unsuccessful.

Apart from the fees in accordance with Subsections 1 and 3 the cash expenses are to be paid, in particular:

1) travelling expenses of officials,
2) fees paid to witnesses and experts,
3) clerical expenses.

Fees for witnesses and experts are to be calculated in accordance with the *Statute Regarding the Fees for Witnesses and Experts* (R.G. Bl., 1898, 689).

A lump sum is to be determined for all expenses other than those specified in Subsection 4, Nos. 1 to 3.

In the case of government enterprises the fee specified in Subsection 1 shall not be paid.

Section 26

The District Commissioner is to determine the amount of costs and the person liable to pay in a separate decision after the compensation has been finally determined.

The District Commissioner can beforehand request the entrepreneur to pay an appropriate advance on costs, cautioning him that the expropriation procedure would be suspended at his expense if no payment were made within a set period.

If the same costs are owed by several persons, they will be liable as joint debtors.

Decisions reached in accordance with Subsections 1 and 2 can be appealed against by any of the parties concerned by lodging an objection with the Governor within a month of their being served.

Objections shall not delay the execution of the decision. The District Commissioner and the Governor can direct that the execution of a decision against which an objection has been lodged be postponed.

VI. Witnesses and experts

Section 27

The provisions in the *Statute Regarding Civil Procedures* regarding proof obtained from witnesses and experts are, with the following provisos, applicable to calling and examining witnesses and experts.

Any person holding a right which is affected by an expropriation order is to be regarded as a 'party' in the meaning of the *Statute Regarding Civil Procedures.*

Notwithstanding Sections 393 and 402 of the *Statute Regarding Civil Procedures,* the examining authority shall be free to decide whether or not to put a witness or expert under oath. The oath is to be administered after the examination is closed.

The examining authority shall determine whether the evidence given by a witness or expert is to be given in writing, or orally and recorded during the hearing. If confirmation by oath is ordered, the evidence should be given orally before the authority and recorded; the authority is to call in a recorder.

A fine imposed on a witness or expert because he fails to attend, or refuses to give evidence or an opinion, cannot be commuted to imprisonment. Should there be a repeated refusal, only the fine permissible for cases of first refusal can be reimposed; there shall be no other coercive measures. The penalties shall be executed by order of the authority which imposed them. Section 26, Subsection 4 and 5 are correspondingly applicable.

VII. Notices

Section 28

Documents are to be served by registered mail (telegram), or by delivering the original or a certified copy of the document to be served.

The authority instigating the service is entitled to use officials in its employ to certify or to deliver documents; it can also effect delivery by requesting another authority in the Protectorate to do so.

Section 170, Subsection 1 and Sections 171 to 173, 180 to 184, 186, 189 of the *Statute Regarding Civil Procedures* are correspondingly applicable to documents which are served by means of delivery. The manner, place and date of delivery must be recorded in the files.

Delivery by means of registered mail to the German Reich shall be made in exchange for a return-certificate.

If documents are to be served abroad, the Governor shall determine in each individual case the date at which the service is deemed to have taken place. In cases where, according to Sections 21 to 24, the procedure takes place before the District Commissioner, he shall determine this date. The Governor can order that the date is to be determined by the District Commissioner in other cases also.

Section 29

If a party concerned lives outside the district of the District Officer who is competent to conduct the expropriation procedure, the latter can instruct the party to authorise, by a set date, a person living in the district to have documents served on him. If the party does not follow the instruction, that party does not have to be included in subsequent procedures. The instruction should include a warning as to this consequence.

Section 30

Where the beginning of a set period depends on a public notice, the first notice of this kind shall be decisive. Subsequent notifications must refer to the first.

VIII. Competence

The District Commissioner in whose district the land is situated which, or a right to which, is to be expropriated shall be competent to conduct the expropriation procedure. If the land is situated in several districts, the Governor shall determine which District Commissioner is competent; he can also direct that the procedure be divided between the districts.

For areas which do not belong to a District Office the Chancellor of the Reich (Foreign Office, Colonial Section) shall determine which authority shall exercise the powers given to District Commissioners in this Ordinance.

The Chancellor of the Reich shall, in general, be empowered to regulate the competence of authorities for the conduct of expropriation procedures in individual Protectorates in departure from this Ordinance.

IX. Special Regulations for the Protection of Native Rights of Ownership and Possession of Land

Section 32

Apart from cases covered by Section 1, the Chancellor of the Reich shall be empowered to permit the expropriation of land which has passed from the dominion or possession of natives to non-natives, for the purpose of reinstating natives in possession, in so far as the expropriation is necessary, according to the discretion of the authorities, to ensure the possibility of an economic livelihood for the natives and in particular their right to a home.

Compensation to those owning or possessing such land at the time shall be paid by the Treasury of the Protectorate. The compensation can be limited to a refund of the costs of the original acquisition of the land from the natives.

The expropriated land shall become, as crown land, the property of the Treasury of the Protectorate, which leaves the use of the land to the natives.

The Chancellor of the Reich shall determine in each case the details of the procedure, acting on a report from the Governor. The Governor shall be empowered to make an interim decision on the question of possession until this order has been issued. He can delegate this power to another authority.

X. Final Provisions

Section 33

The special regulations regarding the resumption or restriction of real property for purposes of mining are not affected by this Ordinance.

Section 24

This Ordinance shall come into force on 1st June 1903.

At the same time the following statutory provisions shall be repealed: the *Ordinance of the Imperial Governor of German East Africa Regarding the*

Expropriation of Real Property, of 15th January 1894 (D.K. Bl., 1894, 270), Section 8 of the *Ordinance of the Governor of the Cameroons Regarding the Acquisition, the Loss and the Restrictions of Real Property,* of 27th March 1888, and the *Ordinance of the Imperial Governor of German South-West Africa Regarding the Acquisition of Land along the Swakopmund–Windhuk Railway Line,* of 24th September 1901 (D.K. Bl., 1902, 4).

Executed with our own hand and under the Imperial Seal.
Given at Berlin, 14th February 1903.

(L.S.)

Wilhelm
Graf v. Bülow

IMPLEMENTATION ORDER OF THE CHANCELLOR OF THE REICH FOR PART IX OF THE IMPERIAL ORDINANCE REGARDING THE EXPROPRIATION OF REAL PROPERTY IN THE AFRICAN AND PACIFIC PROTECTORATES, OF 14th FEBRUARY 1903, OF 12th NOVEMBER 1903*

By virtue of the power to permit, under certain conditions, the expropriation of land which has passed from the dominion or possession of natives to non-natives for the purpose of reinstating the natives in possession to ensure the possibility of their economic livelihood and in particular their right to a home, as granted to the Chancellor of the Reich in Section 32[1] (Part IX) of the *Imperial Ordinance Regarding the Expropriation of Real Property in the African and Pacific Protectorates,* of 14th February 1903, I hereby order as follows:

Section 1

A written declaration by the Governor (Administrator) that the special provisions of Section 32 of the said Imperial Ordinance of 14th February 1903 are not applicable to a certain block of land, also precludes any other manner of expropriation in accordance with the general provisions contained in Parts I to VIII and X of this Ordinance or other provisions taking their place.

The declaration (Subsection 1) can also refer to groups of blocks of land.

The declaration is final.

Section 2

Any non-native claiming ownership of land is entitled to apply at any time to the Governor for a declaration of the kind defined in Section 1.

The application can be combined with a further application to set aside, prior to issuing the declaration, those areas of land whose expropriation, according to the authorities, may be required in favour of natives in accordance with Section 32 of the Imperial Ordinance of 14th February 1903, and

---

* D.K.G., Vol. 7, 236-8.

1 The German original says Section '22' instead of Section '23' but this is clearly a printing error as Section 22 is included in Part IV (and not IX) and also deals with a different matter.

to determine an appropriate compensation for the cession of those areas in agreement with the applicant.

Section 3

The Governor is to comply with the application for a declaration of the kind defined in Section 1:

1. if he knows that no substantiated legal or equitable claims to the land are held by natives,
2. if an amicable settlement between the claims of the applicant and those of natives has been reached in the presence of the authorities,
3. if the application is made with reference to:
   a) blocks of land which have been registered after a public notice since the *Imperial Ordinance Regarding the Rights to Land in the German Protectorates*, of 21st November 1902 (R.G. Bl., 1902, 183) became effective,
   b) blocks of land which have been entered into the Land Register of the former Superior Court in Samoa in accordance with Section 4 of the *General Act of the Samoa Conference in Berlin*, of 14th June 1889,
   c) blocks of land which have been transferred by one of the Treasuries of the African Protectorates,
   d) parts of blocks of land which have not been inhabited or cultivated by natives within the last five years before this Order becomes effective,
   e) parts of blocks of land, which non-natives have acquired in good faith and which they have inhabited or cultivated for three years without objections on the part of the authorities.

Section 4

If the Governor thinks that he cannot comply with an application for a declaration of the kind defined in Section 1, he must report the matter without delay to the Chancellor of the Reich, stating the details of the case. Following this report the Chancellor of the Reich shall either instruct the Governor to issue the declaration applied for, or to instigate expropriation procedures in accordance with Section 32 of the Imperial Ordinance of 14th February 1903.

Section 5

If expropriation procedures are instituted, the areas to be expropriated shall be determined by Land Commissions in corresponding application of the provisions made in Sections 3 and 4 of the *Crown Land Ordinance for the*

Cameroons, of 15th June 1896 (D.K. Bl., 1896, 435) for land to be set aside in favour of natives when crown land is occupied and for Land Commissions to be established to investigate and declare crown land.

The Chancellor of the Reich shall determine the compensation to be paid to the present owner, following a report from the Governor after the parties concerned have been heard.

The principles of equity are to be applied.

Section 6

The Government shall keep lists of the declarations of the kind defined in Section 1. They may be inspected under the same conditions as the Ground Book.

A certified copy of the entry is to be added to the Ground Book (Land Register) files.

Section 7

The procedure in accordance with this Order is free of charge

Section 8

This Order shall come into force on 1st January 1904.

Berlin, 12th November 1903.

The Chancellor of the Reich
Graf. v. Bülow

BIBLIOGRAPHICAL NOTES

BIBLIOGRAPHICAL NOTES

BIBLIOGRAPHICAL NOTES

These notes refer to additional published and unpublished material – in particular in English – which could be helpful in using this collection of documents. The survey is by no means exhaustive. The most convenient location of the material in question has been added in brackets, unless there is clearly no difficulty. The convenience is judged from the point of view of a user situated in Papua New Guinea.

A. Legislation

The German colonial laws applying in New Guinea were published in the following official periodicals:

1. *Nachrichten über Kaiser Wilhelms-Land und den Bismarck-Archipel* (published by the Neu Guinea Kompagnie), Berlin, 1885-1898 (U.P. N.G.).
2. *Amtsblatt für das Schutzgebiet Deutsch Neuguinea* (published by the Imperial Government of German New Guinea), Rabaul, 1909-1914 (M.L.).
3. *Deutsches Kolonialblatt, Amtsblatt für die Schutzgebiete in Afrika und der Südsee* (published by the German Colonial Office), Berlin, 1890-1921 (U.P.N.G.).

As pointed out in the text (see *Contents*, Nos. 9, 10, 14-18) the general conditions for the transfer of government land, contract forms etc. were not included in these publications. For this reason photocopies of those included in this collection have been deposited in the Supreme Court Library in Port Moresby.

There exist a number of official and unofficial collections of German colonial laws. The following two were prepared in German New Guinea:

4. *Auszugsweise Zusammenstellung der wichtigsten in Deutsch-Neu-Guinea (Bismarck-Archipel, Deutsche Salomons-Inseln und Kaiser Wilhelmsland) geltenden Verordnungen (abgeschlossen im September 1903)* (published by the Imperial Government of German New Guinea), Berlin, 1903 (H.W.W.A.).
5. *Sammlung von in Deutsch Neu Guinea und dem Inselgebiet geltenden Gesetzen, Verordnungen und dergleichen (Stand vom 1.1.1912)* (published by the Imperial Government of German New Guinea), Rabaul, 1912 (N.L.).

The most important of the general collections of German colonial law is:

6. Riebow, Zimmermann (*et al.*) (eds.) *Die deutsche Kolonialgesetzgebung, Sammlung der auf die deutschen Schutzgebiete bezüglichen Gesetze, Verordnungen, Erlasse und internationalen Vereinbarungen, mit Anmerkungen und Sachregister,* 13 vols., Berlin, 1893-1910 (covering the period up to 1909) (N.L.).

The official publication of the metropolitan legislation to which it refers was effected in:

7. Gesetzes-Sammlung für die Königlichen Preussischen Staaten (*Preussische Gesetzes-Sammlung*) (published by the Prussian Government), Berlin (N.L., incomplete).
8. *Reichsgesetzblatt* (published by the Government of the Reich), Berlin (N.L.).

One of the best known private collections of German/Prussian law is:

9. Grotefend, G.A. (ed.) *Die Gesetze und Verordnungen für den Preussischen Staat und das Deutsche Reich,* 3 vols., Berlin, 1884 (covering the period between 1806 and 1884.

The title was later changed to:

10. Grotefend, G.A. [and E. Cretschmar – from 1895] *Das gesamte preussisch-deutsche Gesetzgebungsmaterial,* Berlin (yearly since 1885).

This collection (and many other of the German works mentioned here) were held by the German Court Library in Rabaul. Contrary to a widely held belief this library was not completely destroyed during World War II. A substantial part of it, including most relevant volumes of the Grotefend collection, are at present housed in the National Library of Australia, Canberra.

We are not aware of any published English translations of German colonial laws. In the New Guinea context a number of unpublished translations of individual pieces of legislation were prepared at various times – for instance for use in individual court cases – but they are usually not very satisfactory and are, in any case, mostly concerned with documents also translated in this collection.

With regard to the relevant German metropolitan land law the situation is slightly better.

There exists at least one translation of the German *Civil Code:*

11. Chung Hui Wang, *The German Civil Code; translated and annotated with an Historical Introduction,* London, 1907 (N.L.).

We have not been able to find an English translation of the Prussian land statutes of 1872.

B. Judicial Decisions

Decisions by courts in German New Guinea were not officially reported. The court files (in so far as they survived) are still housed in the Australian Commonwealth Archives in Canberra, although negotiations regarding their transfer to the National Archives of Papua New Guinea are under way.[1] It is hoped that it will be possible to publish some of these decisions at a later date.

The decisions of Australian courts in New Guinea between the two World Wars were also not officially reported. However, the three surviving major decisions of Mr Justice Phillips in land cases (*Re Jomba Plain, Re Malala* and *Re Mortlock Islands*) were included in the 1971-72 volume of the *Papua New Guinea Law Reports* (501-657).

Of these *Re Mortlock Islands* is of special significance as it contains a tentative summary of much of the German land legislation in New Guinea (ibid. 635-44) – although Mr Justice Phillips was not prepared to give a decision on the only specific question involving German colonial law before him "because the translations of the German laws before the court were made by one who did not have the legal training to translate German legal terms into English legal terms" (ibid. 622). The importance of the other two decisions is historical rather than legal; they contain the only detailed descriptions of early European land acquisitions compiled at a time when the German land files were still in existence.

12. *Custodian of Expropriated Property* v. *Commissioner of Native Affairs* (*Re Jomba Plain*) (1932) [1971-1972] P. & N.G.L.R. 501-89.
13. *Custodian of Expropriated Property* v. *Commissioner of Native Affairs* (*Re Malala*) (1932) [1971-1972] P. & N.G.L.R. 590-618.
14. *Custodian of Expropriated Property and Phoebe Kroening* v. *Commissioner of Native Affairs* (*Re Mortlock Islands*) (1930) [1971-1972] P. & N.G.L.R. 621-57.

Some years after World War II a Council of Law Reporting for the Territory of Papua and New Guinea was finally established, and the first volume of the *Papua [and] New Guinea Law Reports* was published in 1963.

The Reports included a number of Supreme Court decisions in land matters, usually land titles restoration cases on appeal from the Land Titles Commission whose decisions are not reported. However, the need for considering questions of German colonial land law in the context of land titles restoration proceedings was rather limited, especially after the decision of the

[1] Copies of German judicial decisions have also survived in the files of the German Colonial Office, now held by the Central Archives in Potsdam.

High Court of Australia in *Custodian of Expropriated Property* v. *Tedep (Re Varzin Lands)* (1964) 113 C.L.R.318[1] – and, one must add, the eagerness to do so was, understandably, none too great. As a result these decisions are of comparatively little assistance in understanding German colonial land law in New Guinea. The following decisions are the most rewarding among those reported.

15. *Tolililu and Tolikun* v. *Director of Native Affairs (Re Sulka Native Reserve)* (1963, Ollerenshaw, A.C.J.) [1965-66] P. & N.G.L.R. 12-41.
16. *Tolain and Others* v. *The Administration of the Territory of Papua and New Guinea (Re Vulcan Land)* (1966. Minogue J.) [1965-66] P. & N.G.L.R. 232-78.
17. *Custodian of Expropriated Property* v. *Director of District Administration (Re Wangaramut)* [No.1] (1969, Clarkson J.) [1969-70] P. & N.G.L.R. 133-64.
18. *Director of District Administration* v. *Custodian of Expropriated Property (Re Wangaramut)* [No.2] (1970, Minogue and Frost J.J., O'Loghlen A.-J.) [1969-70] P. & N.G.L.R. 410-56.
19. *The Administration of the Territory of Papua and New Guinea* v. *Blasius Tirupia and Others (Re Vunapaladig and Japalik Land)* (1971 Minogue C.J., Clarkson and Kelly J.J.) [1971-1972] P. & N.G.L.R. 229-46.
20. *The Director of Native Affairs* v. *The Custodian of Expropriated Property (Re Adolfhafen Virgin Land)* (1971, Frost S.P.J.) [1971-1972] *P. & N.G.L.R. 326-39.*

C. Literature

Despite the short duration of the German Colonial Empire the German literature on colonial law is quite extensive -- but it would be pointless to include a comprehensive list of items dealing with German colonial land law. A detailed bibliography is contained in:

21. Schack, F. *Das Deutsche Kolonialrecht in seiner Entwicklung bis zum Weltkriege,* Hamburg, 1923 (A.N.U.).

---

1 See also *Nambumutka Simbali* v. *Sacred Heart Mission (New Britain) Property Trust (Re Toriu)* (1973) 47 A.L.J.R. 666.

The only text-book is:

22. Pink, L. and G. Hirschberg. *Das Liegenschaftsrecht in den deutschen Schutzgebieten,* Band I: Das Grundstücksrecht, Berlin, 1912 (A.N.U.).

There exists one contemporary article dealing specifically with land in German New Guinea:

23. Wolff, E. Das Recht am Grund und Boden im Schutzgebiet von Deutsch Neuguinea, *Zeitschrift für Kolonialpolitik,* Vol.8 (1906) 464-504 (U.P.N.G.).

The literature in English dealing with German colonial land law in New Guinea is naturally very limited. Some information is contained in:

24. Mackenzie, S.S. *The Australians at Rabaul* (Vol.10 of The Official History of Australia in the War of 1914-1918), Sydney, 1937 (U.P.N.G.).
25. Mair, L.P. *Australia in New Guinea,* London, 1948 (U.P.N.G.).
26. Rowley, C.D. *The Australians in German New Guinea 1914-1921,* Melbourne, 1958 (U.P.N.G.).

The only book concentrating on land questions in German New Guinea is:

27. Sack, P.G. *Land Between Two Laws,* Canberra, 1973 (U.P.N.G.).
but it has a strong historical emphasis and is not concerned with the technical aspects of colonial land law.

We are not competent to say what literature on German metropolitan land law either written in or translated into English is available.[1] Judging by the holdings in Canberra and in the library of the Max-Planck-Institut für Ausländisches und Internationales Privatrecht in Hamburg it is extremely limited. The following books are probably the most useful:

28. Huebner, R. *A History of Germanic Private Law* (Translated by F.S. Philbrick) Boston, 1918 (A.N.U.).
29. Schuster, E.J. *The Principles of German Civil Law,* Oxford, 1907 (A.N.U.).
30. *Manual of German Law,* 2 vols., 2nd ed., British Institute of International and Comparative Law Series, Nos. 14-15, 1968-71 (U.P.N.G.).

[1] The literature in German is, naturally, quite overwhelming.

INDEXES AND GLOSSARY

Indexes and Glossary

When we began to compile the subject index for this collection, we felt tempted to smuggle in at least some of the explanations we had discussed while working on the translations. As it was clear from the outset that to achieve an adequate coverage the explanatory notes would have to run into several hundred pages, we were again faced with the unpleasant necessity of having to choose the least unsatisfactory of compromises.

Mainly to soothe our conscience, we decided to add a glossary of some technical German terms, combined with brief explanatory notes on the administrative organisation of German New Guinea and the types of legal documents included in this collection (pp.105ff.). As can be seen from the glossary, no attempt has been made to deal with the concepts of German land law, as this would have required detailed commentaries – whereas superficiality in marginal areas seemed to be excusable.

It proved impossible to compile a consistent subject index (pp.110ff.) which abandoned the system of the German legislation and listed instead, for example, the headings a Papua New Guinea lawyer was most likely to look for. Further, it must be stressed that the index is, for several reasons, far from complete. There did not appear to be much point in splitting the entries relating, for instance, to the registration of land too far, as most of the relevant subject matter is regulated in legislation not included in this collection. On the other hand, the documents included deal not only with land, but also with very different matters, such as the change-over from Neu Guinea Kompagnie to Reich coins. Such matters have been excluded from the subject index.

The index of statutes, ordinances etc. referred to in this collection (pp.114ff.) gives some idea of the body of legal documents which would have to be translated before all the law relevant to land in German New Guinea would be available in English.

The list of place names (pp.119f.) has been thrown in for good measure and because it ties the documents to the topography of Papua New Guinea instead of letting them drift in a remote and cloudy legal sky. It is meant to be self-explanatory, although geographical names in Papua New Guinea always present problems. But as we felt the search for any solutions was clearly outside our province, these problems did not worry us over much.

I. GLOSSARY OF SOME TECHNICAL TERMS

A. Note on the administrative organisation of German New Guinea

This note indicates how the various officials and bodies mentioned in the documents fit into the administrative hierarchies which governed German New Guinea at various times.

At the top of the hierarchies was always the Reich in which the sovereignty over German New Guinea (*Oberhoheit*) was vested. Between 1885 and 1899 the local sovereignty (*Landeshoheit*) was exercised by the Neu Guinea Kompagnie, which was during this period the *Landesverwaltung* (Administration). In 1899 it was replaced in this capacity by the *Kaiserliche Gouvernement* (Imperial Government).

German law distinguishes the State in its capacity as sovereign (administrative authority) from the State in its capacity as holder of private rights and duties. In this latter capacity it is constructed as a separate legal person: the *Fiskus*, which is roughly the equivalent of the Treasury. In the case of the Neu Guinea Kompagnie as local sovereign this separate legal person was not necessary; the Company as a commercial enterprise was its own *'Fiskus'*. For the period after 1899 it is necessary to distinguish between the *Reichsfiskus* (Treasury of the Reich) and the *Landesfiskus* (the Treasury of German New Guinea). Hence there are two alternative double hierarchies: the Reich and the Treasury of the Reich, and either: the Administration and the Neu Guinea Kompagnie, or: the Imperial Government and the Treasury of German New Guinea.

In colonial matters the Reich was represented by the *Kaiser* (Emperor), who delegated most of his powers to the *Reichskanzler* (Chancellor of the Reich) as head of the *Reichsregierung* (German Government). Until 1907 most of the actual colonial administration in Berlin was carried out by the *Kolonial Abteilung des Auswärtigen Amtes* (the Colonial Section of the Foreign Office), which then became – as *Reichs-Kolonial-Amt* (German Colonial Office) – a separate department; only the German possessions in China were administered by the *Reichs-Marine-Amt* (German Naval Office).

Although the Emperor was entitled to enact colonial legislation, the legislative bodies of the Reich, *Reichstag* (Parliament) and *Bundesrat* (the Federal Council, representing the Governments of the German States) were also involved. The various German colonies had no independent legislative bodies; the development of representative government, even in the form of local government, was only just beginning. The general colonial legislation mentions local government (*Gemeindevertretung*), but in German New Guinea only an Advisory Council (*Gouvernementsrat*) had been established.

As far as the colonial administration in German New Guinea itself is concerned, four periods must be distinguished. At first there was only an Imperial Commissioner (*Kaiserlicher Kommissar*), whose functions were still very much like those of a Consul General. (For some years before his arrival purely consular functions had already been exercised by a non-professional consul.) The Imperial Commissioner was then replaced by the *Landeshauptmann* (Administrator) of the Neu Guinea Kompagnie, who was responsible to the Company, represented by a Board of Directors (*Direktion*), headed by a Chairman (*Vorsitzender*). German New Guinea was divided into administrative districts (*Stationsbezirke*), and a Station Manager (*Stationsvorsteher*) was in charge of each of them. Between 1889 and 1892 the *Landeshauptmann* was again replaced by an Imperial Commissioner who was assisted by an Imperial Chancellor (*Kaiserlicher Kanzler*), who was a kind of Deputy-Administrator for the Bismarck Archipelago, a role which was later taken over by the Imperial Judge (*Kaiserlicher Richter*) for the Bismarck Archipelago.

In 1899 the Administrator was replaced by an Imperial Governor (*Kaiserlicher Gouverneur*) who headed an Imperial Government (*Kaiserliches Gouvernement or Kaiserliche Regierung*). A Vice-Governor (*Vize-Gouverneur*) was in charge of the semi-independent 'Island Territory' which was then added to German New Guinea. The 'Old Protectorate' was divided into administrative districts, which, depending on importance, were administered either by a *Bezirksamtmam* (District Commissioner) or a *Stationschef* or *Stationsleiter* (District Officer). The District Officer was usually directly responsible to the Governor and not to a District Commissioner.

Judicial and administrative functions were rarely separated in German New Guinea. The Administrator (Imperial Commissioner, Imperial Governor) was at the same time the Superior Judge (*Oberrichter*), and most District Commissioners or District Officers (Station Managers) were simultaneously in charge of a District Court (*Bezirksgericht*) or Station Court (*Stationsgericht*). Further, the District Court was also the land registration office (*Grundbuchamt* or *Grundbuchbehörde*) over which the Judge of the District Court (*Bezirksrichter*) presided as *Grundbuchrichter* (Ground Book Judge).

B. Note on types of German legal documents

German law distinguishes between a *Gesetz* (Statute), passed by the legislature, on the one hand, and a *Verordnung* (Ordinance) or *Verfügung* (Order), issued by the executive (by virtue of a statutory authority), on the other. It is difficult to define the difference between a *Verordnung* and a *Verfügung*. Other similar terms are also used (for instance: *Erlass* (decree) or *Bestimmung* (regulation). The term *Gesetz*, too, is sometimes modified or replaced (for instance: *Bürgerliches Gesetzbuch* (Civil Code) – instead of *Bürgerliches Gesetz*, *Grundbuchordnung* (Ground Book Act) – instead of *Grundbuchgesetz*, or *Preussisches Allgemeines Landrecht* (Prussian Common Law) – instead of *Preussisches Allgemeines Landgesetz*).

There are two related types of subsidiary legislation which can take the form of a statute or ordinance etc.: legislation to introduce (*einführen*) or implement (*ausführen*) other legislation (hence: *Einführungsgesetz* (Statute introducing ...), *Ausführungsverfügung* (Implementation Order) etc.).

Further, this collection includes documents from areas where legislation merges either with contracts or with administrative acts. The latter usually take the form of internal instructions to officials (*Anweisungen* (Instructions or Directions) or, more precisely, *Dienstanweisungen* (Internal Administrative Instructions)), the former that of general conditions for the conclusion of contracts (*Allgemeine Bedingungen* (General Conditions), *Geschäftsbedingungen* (Conditions of Contract) or *Allgemeine Grundsätze* (General Principles)).

The *Schutzbrief* (Charter or Letter of Protection) is closely related to an administrative act, but leads, at the same time, to the area of international agreements, which can result in an *Erklärung* (Declaration) or even an *Akt* (Act) – a term otherwise now mainly used for executive acts (*Verwaltungsakt* (Administrative Act), *Hoheitsakt* (Sovereign Act)), and not for legislative or contractual acts.

Finally there are the printed forms for contracts and other legal dealings and the individual contract between the Reich and the Neu Guinea Kompagnie which reversed the situation created by the Imperial Charters.

Allgemeine Bedingungen	General Conditions
Amtliche Bekanntmachung	Official (Public) Notice
Anweisung	Direction or Instruction
Ausführungsverfügung	Implementation Order
Auswärtiges Amt (Kolonial Abteilung)	Foreign Office (Colonial Section)
Bezirksamt	District Office
Bezirksamtmann	District Commissioner
Bezirksgericht	District Court
Bezirksrichter	District Court Judge
Bundesrat	Federal Council
Bürgerliches Gesetzbuch	(German) Civil Code
Dienstanweisung	Internal Administrative Instruction
Direktion	Board of Directors
Einführungsgesetz	Statute Introducing...
Erklärung	Declaration
Erlass	Decree
Fiskus	Treasury
Geheimer Kommerzienrat	Privy Councillor for Commerce
Gesetz	Statute
Gouvernementsrat	Advisory Council
Grundbuchamt (Grundbuchbehörde)	Ground Book Office
Grundbuchordnung	Ground Book Act
Grundbuchrichter	Ground Book Judge
Grundsätze	Principles
Kaiser	Emperor
Kaiserlicher Gouverneur	Imperial Governor
Kaiserlicher Kanzler	Imperial Chancellor
Kaiserlicher Kommissar	Imperial Commissioner
Kaiserlicher Richter	Imperial Judge
Kaiserliches Gouvernement (Kaiserliche Regierung)	Imperial Government
Landesfiskus	Treasury of the State (or Colony)
Landeshauptmann	Administrator
Landeshoheit	Local Sovereignty
Landesverwaltung	Administration of the State (or Colony)
Oberhoheit	Supreme Sovereignty
Oberrichter	Superior Judge
Öffentliche Bekanntmachung	Public Notice
Preussisches Allgemeines Landrecht	Prussian Common Law

Reichsfiskus	Treasury of the Reich[1]
Reichskanzler	Chancellor of the Reich
Reichs-Kolonial-Amt	Colonial Office of the Reich
Reichs-Marine-Amt	Naval Office of the Reich
Reichsregierung	Government of the Reich
Reichstag	Parliament of the Reich
Schutzbrief	Charter
Station	Station
Stationschef (Stationsleiter)	District Officer
Stationsgericht	Station Court
Stationsvorsteher	Station Manager
Stellvertretender Gouverneur	Acting Governor
Verfügung	Order
Verordnung	Ordinance
Vize-Gouverneur	Vice-Governor
Vorsitzender	Chairman

1 For the sake of convenience 'Reich' and 'German' have been treated as synonymous in the text (i.e. Colonial Office of the Reich = German Colonial Office).

II. Subject Index

III. INDEX OF STATUTES, ORDINANCES ETC. REFERRED TO IN THIS COLLECTION[1]

A. International Agreements

B. German Metropolitan Law

---

1 Documents included in this collection are marked with an asterisk; the first page reference added in brackets refers to the pages of this collection where the document is reproduced.

E. **Other German Colonies**

IV. INDEX OF PLACE NAMES REFERRED TO IN THIS COLLECTION

www.ingramcontent.com/pod-product-compliance
Lightning Source LLC
Jackson TN
JSHW070937170926
108273JS00020B/29
* 9 7 8 9 9 8 0 8 7 9 1 1 0 *